For Penny & Addison Ellis
with best wishes,
Janet Fox

For the best friends I've ever had.
You've been there for me in the
good and the bad. I treasure
your friendship like no other
Bettye

Winston-Salem
A Cooperative Spirit

By Janet Fox

❖

Corporate Profiles by Bettye Neff

Winston-Salem: A Cooperative Spirit

❖

Produced in cooperation with
Old Salem Inc.
Post Office Box F, Salem Station
Winston-Salem, North Carolina 27108
(910) 721-7300

Community Communications
Montgomery, Alabama

❖

Cover photograph by Murray & Associates

Foreword

While our primary role at Old Salem is to preserve
and interpret life in Salem in the late eighteenth and
early nineteenth centuries, we cannot ignore the greater
context: what came before and what came after. The
Museum of Early Southern Decorative Arts reaches
beyond Old Salem to study and showcase a much broader
region and time period. That, too, does not stand in
a vacuum. As this book goes to press, we are widening
our scope once more by beginning construction of a new
building which will house a special exhibition gallery and
a children's history discovery center. And there is surely
more to come.

The momentum which fuels our growth was born in
the determined nature of those early Moravians who
decided that Salem would be a success long before the
site was even selected. It is the same determined nature
which drives Winston-Salem today.

We are proud to be a part of it, and are pleased to have
a role in presenting *Winston-Salem: A Cooperative Spirit.*

❖

Hobart Cawood
President
Old Salem Inc.

Preface

People who live in Winston-Salem feel, quite rightly, that theirs is a unique city. In trying to tell Winston-Salem's story, I have been impressed, over and over again, with the character that sets this city apart. Its history teaches us that the quality of life we enjoy and take for granted today has not been easily or quickly won. Winston-Salem's history is a chronicle of vision, and the determination and patience and perserverance to make the vision a reality. From the struggles of the first Moravian settlers to civilize the wilderness to the large-spirited efforts to bind people together for the common good today, Winston-Salem has distinguished itself for its aspiration to high ideals and the persistence to achieve them.

Everything distinctive and lasting in Winston-Salem—from the Single Brothers House to Reynolda Gardens to the National Black Theatre Festival—began as an idea in someone's head. I think it must be impossible to write a history without being awed by the individuals whose vision shaped the future. One thing that makes Winston-Salem special is that many daring, ambitious, and innovative ideas have been embraced and carried out by the community as a whole. The preservation of Old Salem, the relocation of Wake Forest University, and the determination to have the North Carolina School of the Arts here are a few examples.

Everyone I have interviewed in my 20 years as a journalist in Winston-Salem, and everyone I have known in my personal and professional life here, has helped to shape this book. I have also relied heavily on the work of the excellent historians that Winston-Salem has produced in abundance. I am grateful to Gene Capps, Dr. William Rice, Langdon Opperman, Richard Murdoch, Joan Dawson, Annette Scippio, Richard Starbuck, and Richard Redding for sharing their knowledge and insight with me. My editor, Lenita Gilreath, has been a constant source of support and encouragement. In this, and in all my endeavors, I have been blessed with the love and faith of the people closest to me, my daughters, Emily and Lucinda Fox, and my husband, Tom Tomlinson.

✛

Janet Fox

Community Communications—Book Division
Publishers: Ronald P. Beers
James E. Turner

Staff for *Winston-Salem: A Cooperative Spirit*
Publisher's Sales Associates: Jeff Brock, Herb Hilliard,
Bill Koons, and Henry Beers
Executive Editor: James E. Turner
Managing Editor: Lenita Gilreath
Design Director: Camille Leonard
Designers: Emily McClure and Katie Bradshaw
Photo Editors: Lenita Gilreath, Emily McClure, and Molly Rawls
Production Assistant: Corinne Cau
Editorial Assistant: Robyn Putz
Proofreader: Wynona Hall
Accounting Services: Sara Ann Turner
Printing Production: Frank Rosenberg/GSAmerica

Community Communications
A Division of LWT Communications Inc.

James E. Turner, Chairman of the Board
Ronald P. Beers, President
Daniel S. Chambliss, Vice President

Table of Contents

Chapter 1

Salem
(1753-1848)

THE HARDY SPIRIT AND
THE STRONG FAITH OF THE
PEOPLE WHO ONCE CALLED
SALEM HOME IS STILL
PRESENT IN THE RESTORED
EIGHTEENTH-CENTURY TOWN.

PHOTO COURTESY OF
OLD SALEM INC.

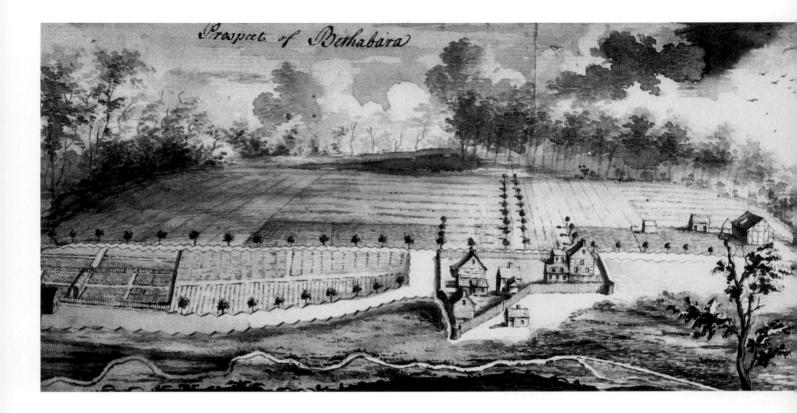

Prospect of Bethabara

To walk through Old Salem today is to get a sense not only of a bygone way of life, but also of the cooperative and peaceful spirit that was the foundation of the modern city of Winston-Salem. Today, this restored eighteenth-century town is the city's premiere visitor attraction, drawing thousands from far and wide to admire its solid and pleasing buildings, its tidy gardens, and demonstrations of the early crafts and customs of the place.

But even in the eighteenth century Salem was a magnet for visitors. They came to stay at its tavern on their journeys and to sip its notable brandy. They came to buy pottery, tools, and food, and to receive medical care. Neighboring families sent their children to its schools.

At a time and in a place where life was rough and harsh, and survival was the highest aspiration for most people, the Salem settlers created a well-ordered, comfortable, prosperous community. What we now call quality of life was a manifest concern of the founders of the town that showed itself in education for all boys and girls,

provisions for the health and safety of all residents, and systems for counseling and helping people facing problems with work, money, and personal relationships. Their buildings, their crafts, their furnishings and landscaping, and the music that was an integral part of their lives all evidenced a love of beauty and enduring quality.

The settlers were members of a Protestant church called *Unitas Fratrum*, or, in English, Unity of the Brethren or United Brethren. They traced their heritage back to John Hus of Bohemia, an early fifteenth-century priest who argued for reform of the Roman church, was declared a heretic, and was burned at the stake. His followers broke from Rome and established a separate church in 1467, well before Martin Luther touched off the Protestant Reformation. The group was almost wiped out in the counter-Reformation wars but was reborn in the early part of the eighteenth century in Germany. There, Nicholas Lewis, Count of Zinzendorf—a lifelong Lutheran—provided sanctuary for a group of religious refugees who came from Moravia and elsewhere to his estate in Saxony. These persecuted people were a mixed lot in terms of their religious backgrounds and nationalities, and they arrived in Saxony with differing ideas of how they wanted to practice their religion. With guidance from Count Zinzendorf, they entered into an agreement of how they would live as a separate community, a model based on the early Christians. There, at Herrnhut, a pattern of social organization was established that the Moravians, as they came to be called, would take to their settlements in America.

They wanted to live in Christian love, to make their daily lives a service of devotion, and to that end they set up rules and practices and customs that would make them seem quite strange to their new neighbors in the sparsely populated North Carolina wilderness, even while others admired their highly civilized community and depended upon their industry. With their history of persecution, they wanted to be safe to live according to their own beliefs, without interference or contamination from outsiders.

One indication of their success is that German remained the official language of the North Carolina Moravian communities well into the 1850s. Moravian "aloofness" was to be a strong component of the character of Winston-Salem, some would say until the present day.

By the time the first Moravians set foot in North Carolina, their reputation for being sober, industrious, desirable colonists had preceded them. The Moravians had come first to Georgia and then had established settlements in Pennsylvania. Lord Granville of England, who owned vast tracts of land in North Carolina, was anxious to see the Moravians established in his territory and offered to sell them some of his land. A small scouting party led by Bishop August Gottlieb Spangenberg left Bethlehem, Pennsylvania, in August 1752, for an expedition through the North Carolina back country, a journey plagued with illness, mosquitoes, terrible weather, and wrong turns. Finally, on January 8, 1753, the little group found what Spangenberg judged to be the best land left in North Carolina, at the place where Muddy Creek splits into three forks. It was a large hilly tract with many springs and streams, forests and meadows, fish and game. What also made it attractive to Bishop Spangenberg—and what had probably made it seem undesirable to other settlers of the North Carolina frontier— was that it was well off the beaten path.

The tract was just short of 100,000 acres, and the Moravian Church was to dominate it for almost 100 years. Spangenberg named it Wachau, or as the Brethren and their neighbors soon began to call it, Wachovia.

An abandoned log cabin was the Moravians' first home in what is now Forsyth County. Eleven carefully selected men from the Pennsylvania communities were the first settlers, including a doctor, a minister, a baker, two carpenters, and a shoemaker. They named the place where they stopped at the cabin Bethabara (House of Passage), and in a matter of months they had built a remarkably self-sufficient town in the middle of nowhere. By the end of 1755, a little over two years from the day the first tree fell, Bethabara had a meeting house, a two-story Single Brothers

BISHOP AUGUST GOTTLIEB SPANGENBERG LED A SMALL SCOUTING PARTY FROM PENNSYLVANIA TO THE NORTH CAROLINA BACK COUNTRY TO FIND THE MORAVIANS A TRACT SUITABLE FOR A SETTLEMENT. SPANGENBERG NAMED THE 100,000-ACRE SITE WACHAU, OR AS THE BRETHREN SOON BEGAN TO CALL IT, WACHOVIA. PHOTO COURTESY OF THE MORAVIAN CHURCH ARCHIVES OF THE SOUTHERN PROVINCE.

FIRST HOUSE IN SALEM, N.C. BUILT 1766.

House, a mill, a tool house, a kiln, a pottery, a tannery, a tailor's shop, seven houses, a smithy, acres of planted crops, and a surrounding palisade.

The temporary House of Passage developed as a close-knit town and trade center perhaps because of Indian raids in the area in the first few years, which inclined people to want to live close together for safety. Food, the presence of a medical doctor, and the protection of the stockade made Bethabara very attractive to non-Moravian visitors. In the years 1757 and 1758 more than 500 people stopped at the settlement, including white settlers and Indians.

But Bethabara was never intended to be the main Moravian settlement, and after a second community had been established at Bethania, three miles away, surveying parties began scrutinizing the entire tract for a suitable site for the town that already had been given a name—Salem.

The choosing of the location is illustrative of how and why the early Moravians did things—and why others considered them distinctly odd. They acted at the behest of the church leaders in Saxony, they went about surveying the land in their very methodical and knowledgeable way, and they left the final choice to the Lord. The way they sought the opinion of their Lord was through the use of the Lot. On serious questions where they felt divine

guidance was needed, the church elders would put slips of paper into a wooden bowl or box. Usually one slip had "ja" written on it, one said "nein," and a third was blank. The question was posed and the Lot was drawn. (Drawing a blank was an indication that the question needed further pondering.) What may sound like fortune telling to modern ears was to the Moravians an expression of humility, an acknowledgment of the limitations of human understanding, and a devout belief in God.

The site chosen in this way was near the center of the Wachovia tract, six miles south of Bethabara. Before the first acre was cleared, the town had been carefully and thoughtfully planned, and a road cut from Bethabara. From the January day in 1766 when the work crew arrived, it would take six years of building before Salem was ready to sustain itself. Much of the labor and materials to build the town had to come from Bethabara and Bethania, which had a combined population of only 219 people. The small team of builders supplemented their labor with hired non-Moravian workmen, and the first two structures erected were log cabins, one for the Brethren, one for the hired hands. These hastily built temporary quarters were nothing like the half-timbered German style buildings that were to come, but one of the original cabins stood for 140 years.

By 1772 Salem, built around an open square, had a *Gemein Haus* for worship services and other gatherings, a Brothers House where unmarried men lived and worked at their trades, a number of solidly built family houses, two farms to provide food for the town, a tavern, a gristmill, a well, a graveyard, and roads, vegetable gardens, and orchards. The main exodus from Bethabara came in that year, and Salem became the manufacturing and commercial center for the Wachovia settlement. In its early days Salem was home to a wide variety of craftsmen and professionals: doctor, apothecary, cabinet maker, carpenter, brickmaker, shoemaker, mason, weaver, miller, wagon maker, metalsmith, distiller, baker, tanner, surveyor, sawyer, and midwife.

One thing that made this eighteenth-century town unusual was how its economic life was arranged. The church owned all the land, and church boards decided which tradesmen could lease property, how much they could charge for their goods, and who they could hire to work for them. The church boards kept a close eye on the quality, productivity, and moral character of the businessmen. Though most of the tradesmen could keep the money they earned, several businesses, including the community store, the tavern, the pottery, the brewery, and the tanyard, belonged to the congregation as a whole, with the profits paid into the community treasury.

The presence of many master craftsmen, strict control of both quality and competition, a habit of industriousness, and, perhaps most of all, the belief that the work of their hands was an expression of their love of God combined to make the Moravian town a prosperous trade center. People came from miles around to buy pottery, guns, saddles,

ON A VISIT TO SEE THE GOVERNOR OF NORTH CAROLINA, PRESIDENT GEORGE WASHINGTON SPENT THE NIGHT IN THE SALEM TAVERN, SHOWN HERE BEFORE RESTORATION. PHOTO COURTESY OF OLD SALEM INC.

OLD SALEM TAVERN.
BUILT 1786.

Sister Elisabeth Oesterlein

✛

Elisabeth Oesterlein was one of a group of 16 girls and women who were selected from the Moravian communities in Pennsylvania to be the first Single Sisters in the settlements in Wachovia. These young women left their families and walked from Bethlehem, Pennsylvania, to Bethabara in 1766—a distance of 500 miles. Elisabeth was 17 years old when she made the trip. The town of Salem was already under construction, but it was not until 1772 that a school was started. Then Elisabeth Oesterlein was appointed teacher of the new Little Girls School. She taught her young pupils reading, writing, and housekeeping skills. She continued teaching until 1780, when she married one of the town's master craftsmen, the potter Rudolph Christ. All of their six children died in infancy, and Elisabeth herself died in 1802. The school continued and thrived and began accepting boarding students as early as 1788. It survives today as Salem College and Academy.

furniture, cloth, and other goods made in Salem, which were of superior quality.

The Brethren also differed from most frontiersmen in their respect for the natural environment. They built their town in the dense woods, and from the earliest days they had a forester who controlled the cutting of trees. Far from regarding the forest as an enemy to be destroyed or beaten back, the Moravians used its poplars for planks, its chestnuts for livestock feed and split-rail fences, its oak for the potter's kiln and to build wagons and houses, its beech for the distiller's fire, its plum and black haw and wild cherry for fruit. From the earth they took clay for bricks, roof tiles, stoves, and the manufacture of their jugs, plates, and bowls. They were adept at making the most of the resources at hand, and a notable example is their creation of one of the first public water-works systems in America. They piped water from springs through hollowed logs joined with iron fittings to the town's tavern, pottery, and tanyard. George Washington was one of many visitors to be impressed with this ingenious arrangement.

As their economic life was arranged by the church, so were the social and private lives of the members structured. Through a system that had been worked out in Herrnhut, each person belonged to a cohort, or "choir," based on age, sex, and marital status. The choirs were Married People, Single Brothers, Single Sisters, Widows, Widowers, Older Boys, Older Girls, Little Boys, and Little Girls. Each group had its own meetings and special festival days and its own responsibilities to the community. The Single Brothers, Single Sisters, and Widows also had their own choir houses, where the members lived and worked together. The choir system gave the church a way of keeping a close watch on the behavior and moral development of each individual. It must also have contributed to the sense of security and belonging and purpose of

ELISABETH OESTERLEIN WAS APPOINTED TEACHER OF THE LITTLE GIRLS SCHOOL IN 1772. THE SCHOOL THRIVED AND BEGAN ACCEPTING BOARDING STUDENTS AS EARLY AS 1788. SHOWN HERE IN 1858, IT SURVIVES TODAY AS SALEM COLLEGE AND ACADEMY. PHOTO COURTESY OF OLD SALEM INC.

WHEN SLAVES WERE PURCHASED BY
THE MORAVIANS, THEY COULD JOIN THE
CONGREGATION IF THEY ACCEPTED
CHRIST AND THE WAYS OF THE
CHURCH. PHOTO COURTESY OF
OLD SALEM INC.

each person. Like the use of the Lot, the choir organization did not stand the test of time, but it did leave a lasting legacy: a concern for the particular needs of people from cradle to grave and a sense of community responsibility for attending to those needs that is still characteristic of Winston-Salem today.

People today wonder at how members of the congregation town could tolerate such strict regulation of their lives. Some of them couldn't. Over the decades dozens of people were expelled from the community, or left of their own accord, because they wanted to marry someone who was not church-approved, or wanted freedom in operating their own businesses. The records are filled with accounts of Salem's citizens being reprimanded and punished for drunkenness, idleness, gossiping, mixing too freely with outsiders, and indulging in unspecified "carnal" infractions.

A self-righteous tone and a sense of moral superiority come through clearly in the voluminous records of the Moravians, an attitude that did not endear them to outsiders. In regard to the peculiar institution that was causing moral anguish to some contemporary religious colonies in America, the Moravians were part of the mainstream in having had no moral objections. They hired slaves as well as free blacks to help build their towns and work in their businesses and farms. Although opposed to individual ownership of slaves, the church began buying slaves in 1769, having discovered that owned, resident workers were a more reliable source of labor than hired, itinerant whites or blacks. In 1790 the first federal census showed that the Moravians in Wachovia owned 40 slaves, while the non-Moravians owned about 50.

The Moravians were known for treating bondsmen more humanely than their neighbors, and some slaves asked to be purchased by the congregations. The Brothers were cautious about slave ownership because they feared that relying on slave labor would make their own members lazy. When slaves were purchased, however, the Moravians extended them the same terms they offered to other outsiders—they could join the congregation if they accepted Christ and the ways of the church. Many blacks did become Moravians. As members of an educated group, they learned to read, and Moravians were holding classes for blacks even after state law forbade it. Blacks had much to contribute to the white Brethren too, in addition to agricultural and diverse work skills they had learned in other places. It is likely that some white Brothers and Sisters learned to speak English from the black people among them.

Traugott Bagge, Merchant

✥

Born into a family of Swedish merchants, educated in the classics and mathematics, experienced in store management, and a convert to the Moravian Church, Traugott Bagge was well equipped to be the manager of Salem's community store. Bagge learned to speak German as a child, and when he was a young man he worked first in his brother's store in Lubeck, Germany, and then in another brother's store in Hamburg. While returning by ship from a buying trip to London in 1753, the young Bagge experienced a rough crossing that caused him to examine his life and to decide that he would join the Moravians. He joined a community of the Brethren in Holland, and later was called to the position of business manager of the Single Brothers in Fulneck, England, where he became proficient in another language that would prove very useful to him, English.

He came to Bethabara in 1768 with his new wife, Rachel Nickelson, and managed the store there while the town of Salem was under construction. The Bagges, with their daughter, were part of the shift from Bethabara to Salem in 1772. The business operated out of temporary quarters until 1775, when the permanent store building in the center of town was completed.

Bagge's job was a big one. He had to procure goods for the store and also tools and supplies for the craftsmen of the town. He was also charged with the trading or selling the commodities the Brethren produced, such as butter, tallow, wheat, and deer skins. Although the townspeople produced most of their own food, clothes, furniture, and utensils, they looked to the store for salt, sugar, coffee, pins and needles, violin strings, curtain rings, buttons, window glass, ribbons, wine, and sundries.

Under Bagge's astute management the store prospered and was a good source of income for the community. In fact, it was well stocked after most country stores in the region were forced to close because of Revolutionary War conditions. Customers flocked to Salem then, but their currency was so depreciated that the Brethren realized they were losing money instead of making profits. As was their custom with thorny problems, the church elders put the question of what to do about the store to the Lord, through the Lot. The advice received was to reduce stock as much as possible.

Brother Bagge was a member of the church board that controlled the business and financial interests of the community. He served as justice of the peace and was as astute in political matters as he was in business affairs. The great sorrow of his life was the loss of his daughter and one of his twin sons to an epidemic of infectious disease. He himself lived to the ripe age of 70, and when he died in 1800 the meeting house could not hold all the Brothers, Sisters, and friends who came to his funeral.

As the name of their central town suggests, the Moravians were peace-loving people. Refusal to bear arms and to swear oaths of allegiance were aspects of their understanding of what it meant to live in accordance with the teachings of Jesus. But colonial America was not an easy place to be a pacifist. The Brothers took up muskets in self-defense during the Indian raids of the 1750s, and their insistence in not getting involved in the Regulators wars a decade later made them the object of suspicion and hostility to people on both sides of those conflicts. More trying times were just ahead.

When colonists up and down the eastern seaboard began chafing against British rule, most of the farmers around the Moravian settlements were on the side of American independence, and by the middle of 1775 they were asking the Moravians for support. The Moravians had received favorable treatment from the British Parliament all along (including exemption from military conscription), and they were still making payments to British landlords. They professed loyalty to King George III, even while they were increasingly sympathetic to and supportive of their patriot neighbors. Traugott Bagge, the manager of Salem's store, supplied the Continental Congress's armies with cloth for uniforms, lead for bullets, food, and other supplies. In trying to remain neutral in the conflict, the Brethren were accused of disloyalty by both sides. The claim to their land was threatened, and all their enterprises suffered from the scarcity of supplies, the worthlessness of the Continental scrip they had to take for their merchandise, and from the dangers of transporting materials and goods through battle zones.

It was a great day for the Moravians when news of the signing of the peace treaty reached them. In 1783 Salem held the first Fourth of July celebration to be proclaimed by a state legislature in the United States. It was a typically

Moravian day of thanksgiving, with a brass band, a lovefeast, a sermon, hymn singing, bell ringing, and a procession of the whole congregation through the town. A similar Independence Day celebration is still held in Salem Square to this day.

Holiday celebrations and traditions are the most visible signs of the early Moravian heritage in modern Winston-Salem. The Moravian congregations of today draw thousands of people of all denominations to their Christmas and Easter observances. The power of music to inspire and unite people is a particularly striking feature of these celebrations.

It is a matter of record that the Brothers celebrated their arrival at the abandoned cabin in Wachovia by composing a hymn of thanksgiving on the spot, and singing it to the accompaniment of wolves howling outside the door. One Brother crafted a trumpet from a tree limb in the first year of the Bethabara settlement, and the men who cleared the first trees for the building of Salem sang as they wielded their axes. Tradition has it that the strange sounds of European musical instruments inside the stockade kept the Indians from ever mounting an attack on Bethabara. In later years it has been said that there isn't a breath of air in Salem that

hasn't been blown through a horn, at least once.

The settlers worked, played, worshipped, greeted visitors, and celebrated significant events in the life of the community to the sound of music, at a time when the Puritans and Calvinists in other parts of colonial America tended to regard instrumental music as the devil's handiwork. The Moravians were the first to bring quantities of instruments to America and the first to use a variety of instruments in their church services. Salem organized a symphony orchestra before 1780, when only two or three other communities in the nation had resident orchestras. Moravian composers produced a significant body of serious music, some of the earliest chamber and choral music to be written in America. Singing, playing, and writing music were, and are still, activities practiced at a high level and enjoyed regularly by many Moravians.

As much a part of the fabric of life as music was the sharing of meals in Christian fellowship. The Moravians called this ritual a lovefeast, and the first lovefeast in Wachovia was held on that first night in the abandoned cabin. The meal then consisted of stewed pumpkin and cornmeal mush. Sweetened, milky coffee and soft buns

IF RELIGION WAS THE CEMENT THAT HELD THE TOWN TOGETHER, MUSIC SERVED AS ITS CHIEF ORNAMENT AND RECREATION. SIGNIFICANT EVENTS IN THE LIFE OF THE MORAVIAN COMMUNITY WERE CELEBRATED TO THE SOUND OF MUSIC. IT HAS BEEN SAID THAT MOST AMERICAN BABIES ARE GIVEN RATTLES TO PLAY WITH; IN SALEM THEY ARE GIVEN TOY TRUMPETS. PHOTO COURTESY OF OLD SALEM INC.

TRAUGOTT BAGGE, MANAGER OF SALEM'S COMMUNITY STORE, CAME TO BETHABARA IN 1768. HE MOVED TO SALEM IN 1772 AND OPERATED HIS BUSINESS OUT OF TEMPORARY QUARTERS UNTIL 1775, WHEN THE PERMANENT BUILDING IN THE CENTER OF TOWN WAS COMPLETED. HIS STORE NOW SERVES AS ONE OF OLD SALEM'S MUSEUM SHOPS. PHOTO COURTESY OF OLD SALEM INC.

THE MORAVIAN ADVENT STAR ORIGINATED IN NIESKY, GERMANY, ABOUT 1850. YEARS LATER PIETER VERBEEK BEGAN MAKING THE STARS TO SELL, AND HIS SON, HARRY VERBEEK, LATER FOUNDED THE HERRNHUT STAR FACTORY. WHEN THE FACTORY CLOSED, GROUPS OF MORAVIANS, IN WINSTON-SALEM AND ELSEWHERE, TOOK UP THE BUSINESS OF PRODUCING THE BELOVED CHRISTMAS SYMBOL. EACH YEAR ON THE FOURTH SUNDAY BEFORE CHRISTMAS, THE STAR IS HUNG IN AREA HOMES AND CHURCHES TO PROCLAIM THE COMING OF CHRIST. PHOTO COURTESY OF OLD SALEM INC.

WHITE STONES OF EQUAL SIZE MARK THE GRAVES OF THE MORAVIAN DEAD. THE INHABITANTS OF GOD'S ACRE ARE BURIED, NOT BY FAMILY, BUT BY CHOIR—GROUPED IN DEATH AS THE EARLY MORAVIANS WERE IN LIFE. PHOTO COURTESY OF OLD SALEM INC.

are the usual lovefeast fare now. They are passed along the pews at the Christmas Eve services held in all Moravian churches. Along with the many-pointed Moravian Advent stars that light up homes in every neighborhood, and the red-paper-trimmed beeswax candles that add a whiff of honey to the deep evergreen scent of the season, the sharing of the lovefeast is a widely cherished way of celebrating Christmas in Winston-Salem.

The custom of holding an Easter sunrise service at the graveyard goes back to the Moravians' years in Herrnhut, and remains unchanged.

In Winston-Salem brass bands go around the city in the dark hours before the morning, waking sleepers with their hymns. Just before dawn the musicians congregate along the street to God's Acre, where rows and rows of white stones of equal size mark the graves of the Moravian dead. At the first ray of sun, a minister of the Church announces the familiar opening words, "The Lord is risen." And the congregation gathered on Salem Square, which usually numbers 10,000, joins in responding, "The Lord is risen indeed!" ❖

Brother Johann Samuel

✛

Sam, a 15-year-old boy, was brought to work as a slave in the stockyard at Bethabara in 1765. The young settlement was lacking members experienced in agriculture and animal husbandry and relied on hired help. The Moravians rented Sam from his owner in Uwharrie, 30 miles away, and within a few years the enslaved youth was chosen to drive a wagon on an expedition to Pennsylvania. He was to work in the stockyard and as a teamster in Bethabara for much of his adult life.

When he was 19, Sam expressed interest in learning to read German, with the idea that he could study the Bible and become a Christian. His owner offered to sell him to the Moravians then, and the church elders put the question of buying a slave to the Lot. The answer came in the affirmative, and Sam was the first slave to be purchased by the Moravians in North Carolina and was taught to read at the Boys School. The Lot was also used in determining that he could be baptized.

On November 13, 1771, hundreds of blacks and whites gathered in the new town of Salem for the consecration of its new *Gemein Haus*. At that same service, Sam was baptized as Johann Samuel, the first black Brother in North Carolina.

Like so many of his white Brethren, Johann Samuel came in for reprimands and punishments from the church elders on several occasions, but he seems to have been a valued member of the community. Especially after most of the residents of Bethabara moved to Salem, he was one of the few experienced farm workers left, and he supervised both black and white Brothers at the communal farm.

In 1780, the church elders decided that Johann Samuel should marry and start a family, to settle him down. There were few prospective brides to choose from, but the church leaders, after long deliberation, decided on Maria, the only baptized Negro woman in Wachovia, who worked at the Salem tavern. Both Johann Samuel and Maria agreed to the arrangement, and they were married and settled in the old Single Brothers House in Bethabara, where Maria took over the communal cooking. Of the seven children born to this first Afro-Moravian couple, four survived. The children went to school in Bethabara, and their oldest daughter joined the Single Sisters choir in Salem and lived in the choir house.

When the communal farm was disbanded in 1800, Johann Samuel was freed, and he and Maria rented a farm near the village. From the beginning he had trouble supporting his family, and Bethabara officials, on several occasions, took note of the bad repair of his house and barn and his failure to make rent payments. Despite all his years of bonded service to them, the Moravians apparently did little to ease his hardship.

In the spring of 1813, the Bethabara diary recorded "a most unpleasant incident" in which the Samuel family was arrested and imprisoned for stealing. A month later Johann Samuel was again arrested, for failing to make a $60 rent payment. The following month the lease on his farm was cancelled and the family ordered to leave.

Banished from the Bethabara congregation, the couple lived out the rest of their lives near Bethania. Church members helped them get established there by buying some of their farm equipment, household goods, and livestock at public auction and then lending it back to the Samuels.

In 1821, the Bethania diary noted that "the Negro Johann Samuel died in our neighborhood." In 55 years in Wachovia, Sam had gone from "Negro" to "Brother" to "Negro," paralleling the Moravians' shifting attitude about race relations.

By this time, the Moravians had become thoroughly Southern in their drive to segregation, and the free and enslaved blacks who had lived and worked among them had separate worship services. The Samuels' two sons were members of the nucleus of the first black Moravian Church in Winston-Salem, Saint Philip's.

Chapter 2

Winston
(1849-1899)

THE FIRST STREETS LAID OUT IN
WINSTON WERE CONTINUATIONS OF
THE MAIN STREETS IN SALEM. UNTIL
1851 THE COUNTY TOWN HAD NO
NAME OTHER THAN SALEM. SHOWN
HERE IS WINSTON'S MAIN STREET,
JUST NORTH OF FOURTH STREET.

PHOTO COURTESY OF THE WACHOVIA
HISTORICAL SOCIETY.

Salem was ordained by God, or so its builders believed. Winston was brought into being by an act of the state legislature. The towns were formally united in 1913, and it is part of Winston-Salem's understanding of its identity that in this merger, two separate traditions were fused. But Winston and Salem were never separated by much more than Salem's long head start.

By 1848 the Moravians in Wachovia had lived in three counties without ever leaving home. As the state's population grew, large counties were divided to create new counties, and Salem businessmen were among those agitating for a division of Stokes County. Forsyth County was carved out of the southern half of Stokes in 1849, and Salem was near its center.

The newly appointed county commissioners, headed by Salem's Francis Fries, were charged with selecting a site and acquiring land for a new county seat. As the land was still in the hands of the Moravian church, a controversy developed, with the conservatives of the congregation favoring a location as far away from Salem as possible and the progressive businessmen assuming that the new county town would be essentially an extension of Salem. The conservative group reflected the old Moravian fear of contamination by outside influences, as was sure to happen if a court house were built under their noses.

The progressive view prevailed, and the 51¼ acres sold for the county seat butted right up against Salem's northern border. The first streets laid out were continuations of the main streets of Salem, and until 1851 the county town had no name other than Salem.

By this time, however, there were as many non-Moravians as Moravians living in Forsyth County. Mostly farmers and slaveholding planters, they were resentful of Moravian dominance and were determined that the county

CHOOSING NOT TO BECOME A MORAVIAN MINISTER, FRANCIS FRIES JOINED A GROUP OF BUSINESSMEN WHO ESTABLISHED THE SALEM COTTON MANUFACTURING COMPANY IN 1835. LATER HE STARTED HIS OWN WOOLEN MILL WITH HIS YOUNGER BROTHER, HENRY, AS A PARTNER. PHOTO COURTESY OF OLD SALEM INC.

seat was not going to be more of the same. Through their efforts the town got a name of its own. It was named for Colonel Joseph Winston, who had been a Revolutionary War hero and later a member of the state legislature and the United States House of Representatives. (Ironically enough, Joseph Winston's landholdings were near the present-day Germanton, still part of Stokes County).

Winston was divided into building lots, which were offered for sale. The first lot was for a public school, which was already in existence. In the years before the Civil War, Winston had few residents. Its dusty little streets did draw crowds for court sessions, political rallies, military drills, and religious revival meetings. People came on foot and horseback and in wagons, and stayed to barter farm produce for manufactured goods in the village stores, camp in the open fields, and gawk at the traveling medicine shows. The music in the air was produced by fiddles and banjos, rather than trombone choirs, and the freewheeling atmosphere was a far cry from the stately pace of Salem.

But Salem was not stuck in the past. During the 1850s most of its traditional structure was dismantled. The church control of trade was abolished, the old lease system was abandoned, the Lot bowl, for all practical purposes, was put away. English became the official language of the church and the primary language of its people, and the town was incorporated.

The crowds got bigger and the political debates more heated after Abraham Lincoln was elected president in 1860. On May 7, 1861, the largest throng ever gathered in Winston to discuss the attack on Fort Sumter and the prospect of North Carolina's secession from the Union. Within days of the state's secession on May 20, the Forsyth Rifles in Salem and the Forsyth Grays in Winston were mobilized. They left for Virginia in June, cheered on by crowds of friends and with God's help in assuring their success and safety publicly beseeched

THE FIRST COUNTY COURTHOUSE, DESIGNED BY FRANCIS FRIES, WAS BUILT IN 1851 AT THE CORNER OF MAIN AND THIRD STREETS. THE COURTHOUSE WAS REBUILT IN 1896 AFTER A FIRE DESTROYED THE ORIGINAL EDIFICE. THE ROMANESQUE STRUCTURE SHOWN HERE WAS DESIGNED BY FRANK P. MILBURN. PHOTO COURTESY OF THE WACHOVIA HISTORICAL SOCIETY.

A GROUP OF PUPILS AT THE SALEM BOYS SCHOOL YARD POSE FOR A NOT-SO-SERIOUS LOOK AT LIFE IN 1896. PHOTO COURTESY OF OLD SALEM INC.

Francis Fries

✛

Francis Levan Fries was Salem's first industrialist, and his career both in business and politics laid the foundation for Winston-Salem's emergence as an industrial and manufacturing center. Born in Salem in 1812, he studied at Nazareth Hall in Pennsylvania to become a Moravian minister. Instead, he joined a group of businessmen who established the Salem Cotton Manufacturing Company in 1835. He made a trip to New England to learn about cotton mill operations, and returned to supervise the construction of Salem's modern, steam-powered mill, which he managed until 1839. He then started his own woolen mill, in which his younger brother Henry later joined him as a partner. Their company, F. and H. Fries Manufacturing Company, was one of the largest textile operations in the South.

Francis Fries served on the committee that drew the boundaries of Forsyth County and was the first chairman of the new county's Board of Commissioners. It was he who arranged for the purchase of land from the Salem congregation for the new county seat, Winston. He also designed its first court house. A few years later, when Salem incorporated as a town, Fries became its mayor and a member of its board of commissioners. He also represented Forsyth County in the state legislature.

The Fries company depended heavily on slave labor, and the family was the largest slaveholder in Salem. When Civil War broke out, the brothers showed none of the old Moravian pacifist tendencies. Their company thrived during the war years, turning out cloth for the Confederate Army.

Francis Fries fathered three sons, all of whom were to be enormously influential in business and public affairs through the years of Winston-Salem's greatest growth. His youngest son, Henry, died at the age of 92 in 1949. Through the century in which these two generations of the Fries family exerted powerful and astute political and economic leadership, they were the living link between Salem's ideal of doing good and Winston industrialists' goal of doing well. They cut the pattern for the power structure Winston-Salem had until recent years.

by the Moravian bishop of Wachovia. When the two companies of young men marched off to war together, Moravian pacifism was the first casualty.

Forsyth County boys spent their first weeks of war at camp in Danville, Virginia, where they wrote home about the good food and sociable evenings of singing, banjo strumming, and card playing. They were soon joined by a third company from home, the Forsyth Southrons. But in July they moved to Manassas Junction, and the grim realities of short rations, exposure to the elements, and deadly typhoid fever set in. More than 30 of the Winston and Salem soldiers died of measles and typhoid in their first months in the Army.

In the next two years, Forsyth men and boys fought and died at Petersburg, Manassas, Fredericksburg, Harper's Ferry, Chancellorsville, Appomattox, and all the major fronts of the bloody conflict. It has been estimated that before it was over, Forsyth County had sent 1,500 soldiers to the Confederacy. Far fewer returned.

At home the mood moved from early support of the war to a growing longing for peace, as shortages of food and other necessities pressed and the death toll mounted. The Fries family, whose mills were working overtime to supply cloth for the Confederate Army and who were large slaveholders, were part of a small but wealthy and influential minority that remained vocal supporters of the war. When Union raiders came through in the spring of 1865, they were joined by crowds of local people in pillaging the Fries' cotton mill.

Many companies were forced out of business by war conditions, but this was a period of growth for one of Salem's oldest institutions, its Girls School. As Northern armies moved into the South, families in every state of the Confederacy began sending their daughters to Salem Female Academy for their safety. The year after the war ended, the academy became chartered as a college.

On February 14, 1872, a bugle call sounded the opening of the first auction sale of leaf tobacco in Winston. The combined population of Winston and Salem was only about 1,200 in that year (Salem being about twice as populous as its young neighbor), and the manufacturing of plug tobacco was but one of a number of small industries being conducted in the community. They included a paper mill, a textile mill, four wagon-making concerns, a carriage-making company, and a flour mill. Little growth had occurred since the end of the Civil War, but that was about to change dramatically. That bugle call, we can say in retrospect, announced the arrival of Winston's towering industry, the source of its wealth, the impetus for its meteoric growth, and the foundation of most of its cultural amenities for a century to come.

The leaf was grown in the area, and with plans underway to connect Winston and Salem to the larger world by laying a track to the Richmond and Danville Railway at Greensboro, the community was poised to become a tobacco manufacturing center. Some of the first to see the potential were two young brothers from neighboring Davie County. Pleasant and John Wesley Hanes built a tobacco factory in 1872, but their lasting contribution to Winston-Salem's economy was to be in textiles. The Hanes tobacco company flourished for a quarter of a century, eventually becoming the third largest seller of tobacco in America. At the turn of the century the brothers sold the company to the man who by then

was determined to emerge as the giant of Winston's giant industry, R. J. Reynolds.

In the quarter century that passed between the day in 1874 when young Richard Joshua Reynolds rode into Winston on horseback, and the day in 1900 when the Hanes brothers sold their interests to him, some 50 tobacco companies sprang up in the town. At the century's end, the tobacco industry was still fragmented, but was clearly dominant. Large family fortunes were established, and so was the pattern of raising capital for expansion within the community. The relationship between the wealthy industrialists and the thousands who worked in their mills and factories—benevolent paternalism on the one hand, and an extraordinary degree of dependency on the other—became firmly entrenched.

Winston was built up fast on the back of its rapidly expanding factories. Unlike the well-planned, careful, controlled development of Salem in the

previous century, Winston sprang up without a master plan. Houses, churches, stores, and public buildings were thrown up around the factories and warehouses, often to be quickly torn down and replaced with bigger structures as the population swelled to meet the demands of industry.

No longer were church elders charting the course for a little community of like-minded people. As thousands of black and white workers poured into Winston, their living conditions, education, health, and prospects were largely determined by the decisions and fortunes of business and industrial leaders.

A fascinating picture of this period, and of how Winston and Salem came to be thoroughly blended, is provided by the Right Reverend Edward Rondthaler. As pastor of Home Moravian Church and a bishop of the Moravian Church, he wrote the Memorabilia of the Salem congregation for 50 years, from 1877 to 1927. (The Memorabilia, annual compilations of noteworthy international,

THE SALEM BRASS BAND MARCHED WITH "THE BLOODY TWENTY-SIXTH" NORTH CAROLINA REGIMENT THROUGH THE CIVIL WAR. THE ALLEGEDLY NEUTRAL MORAVIANS PROCLAIMED SALEM AN "OPEN CITY" DURING THE WAR, BUT UNOFFICIALLY THEIR SYMPATHIES WERE WITH THE SOUTH. WHEN SALEM MEN ENLISTED IN THE CONFEDERATE ARMY, THE TOWN OFFICIALS DID NOT OBJECT. PHOTO COURTESY OF THE WACHOVIA HISTORICAL SOCIETY.

WHEN THE REVEREND EDWARD RONDTHALER CAME TO BE PASTOR OF HOME
MORAVIAN CHURCH IN 1877, HE FOUND TWO SMALL NEIGHBORING TOWNS
STRUGGLING IN THE AFTERMATH OF WAR AND RECONSTRUCTION. IN WRITING THE
ANNUAL MEMORABILIA OF THE CHURCH FOR 50 YEARS, BISHOP RONDTHALER
CHRONICLED THE COOPERATIVE EFFORTS OF SALEM AND WINSTON, THEIR
MERGING, AND THE GROWTH OF WINSTON-SALEM IN THE EARLY TWENTIETH
CENTURY. PHOTO COURTESY OF OLD SALEM INC.

national, local, and congregational
events, are read at the New Year's Eve
service of the church each year).

Having lived in New York and
Philadelphia, Bishop Rondthaler was
clearly struck by the straitened conditions he found in his new home, so
recently ravaged by war, and he was
quick to point out what he thought
would be needed to get the place on its
feet. "In a town situated like ours, with
little of what may be called natural
advantages, a very great deal depends
upon the intelligent enterprise, the thrift,
the steady work, and the friendly cooperation of it citizens," he wrote in the
Memorabilia of 1879. "Every one can
do something, in some way or other, for
the upbuilding of the community."

Rondthaler harkened back to the
founders, who had built up "this favored
community on the edge of the primeval
wilderness." But soon, and increasingly,
cooperation became a persistent theme
in his annual summations, and it was
most often cooperation between Salem
and Winston that he encouraged and
praised.

Cooperation between the business
leaders of Winston and Salem had
begun soon after the end of the War
Between the States, in the effort to get
the much-needed rail connection to
Greensboro. Edward Belo, Israel Lash,
E. A. Vogler, and Henry W. Fries of
Salem joined with Joseph Masten and
Peter and Thomas Wilson of Winston to
raise money for the project. In the
1880s, when it seemed that Winston
was going to lose out to the tobacco
towns of Richmond and Danville in
Virginia if it didn't get more rail lines,
businessmen organized the Roanoke and
Southern Railroad, with Salem's Francis
H. Fries as president, and Winston's
tobacco tycoons R. J. and Will Reynolds
and John and Pleasant Hanes in the
forefront. Forsyth citizens voted bonds
for the railroads, and the tobacco

ON FEBRUARY 14, 1872, A BUGLE CALL SOUNDED THE OPENING OF THE FIRST AUCTION SALE OF LEAF TOBACCO IN WINSTON. THAT BUGLE CALL ANNOUNCED THE ARRIVAL OF WINSTON'S TOWERING INDUSTRY, THE SOURCE OF ITS WEALTH, THE IMPETUS FOR ITS GROWTH, AND THE FOUNDATION OF MOST OF ITS CULTURAL AMENITIES FOR A CENTURY TO COME. PHOTO COURTESY OF THE WACHOVIA HISTORICAL SOCIETY.

manufacturers contributed generously to connect Winston to the larger world. Completion of the railroad to Roanoke was a turning point in the town's fortunes, and the way the $2 million needed to do it was raised can be seen as a model for much of Winston-Salem's community improvement in the century since.

As Rondthaler noted in the Memorabilia of 1888, other towns easily reaped the benefits of railroad companies' decisions to run tracks through them, but Winston and Salem had to struggle and pay for every foot of rail. "Last year we were still confronted with the prospect of being a little town at the end of a little branch road, and the whole business outlook was clouded and discouraged by this fact. The enterprise and public spirit of some of our citizens, supported by the subscription of the township, have materially changed this outlook," the bishop wrote.

By the mid-80s, Winston and Salem were also connected by one Chamber of Commerce, whose first order of business was improving the inadequate access roads to the towns. Among the charter group of directors were the familiar names of Reynolds and Hanes and Fries and Whitaker. It was in this organization that the formal consolidation of Winston and Salem was first proposed, 20 years before the fact.

The establishment of schools and hospitals followed much the same pattern as the building of the railroads. After the Civil War, Forsyth County had 22 one-room public schools. Fewer than a third of school-age children attended them, and the school terms averaged a scant three months. Calvin Wiley, who had been state superintendent of schools before the war, settled in Winston and was a major force in improving public education. When Forsyth County voted itself a tax to supplement the money provided by the state for public education, Wiley was a member of the group of five men (including Pleasant Hanes and James Gray) who worked night after night to plan for Winston's first graded school.

It was called West End School, and the $25,000 it took to get it operating in 1884 was far more than had been raised in the special tax. Private donations from wealthy citizens made up the difference, and West End, one of the first graded schools in the South, brought

THE FIRST SCHOOL FOR BLACKS IN FORSYTH COUNTY, ESTABLISHED SOUTH OF SALEM IN 1867, IS SHOWN IN THIS PHOTOGRAPH BELIEVED TO DATE TO THE LATE 1860S. PHOTO COURTESY OF THE WACHOVIA HISTORICAL SOCIETY.

Winston national acclaim as a leader in the "New South."

Medical care was not a concern of the state in the 1880s, and Winston's first hospital was established entirely with private donations. This time it was the ladies of Winston and Salem who banded together for the good of the community. Thirty-one women formed the Ladies' Twin City Hospital Association in 1887 and raised enough money to open a small, 10-bed hospital in a doctor's house on Liberty Street that same year. It operated for only a few years, and the same women's organization raised money for a bigger hospital in a new building on Brookstown Avenue. More than 3,000 people were treated there before the Twin City Hospital closed its doors

about 1913, and most of them were factory workers and domestic servants, as wealthy people generally were cared for at home when they were sick or injured.

No black students attended West End School, and few black patients were treated at Twin City Hospital, but by the time these institutions came into being, about a third of Winston's population was black. Here, as throughout the South, the races worked together in the factories, but were separated by custom and, in some cases, by law, in education, medical care, housing, and in their churches. The first graded school for black children was longer in coming than the West End School, and for several years the children were taught at classes held in black churches. Depot Street Graded School was built in 1887,

DR. SIMON GREEN ATKINS, SHOWN ON THE FRONT ROW WITH HIS WIFE, WAS THE FOUNDER OF THE SLATER INDUSTRIAL ACADEMY, THE FORERUNNER OF WINSTON-SALEM STATE UNIVERSITY. DR. ATKINS DID MORE THAN ANYONE TO IMPROVE THE PROSPECTS OF WINSTON-SALEM'S LARGE BLACK POPULATION. PHOTO COURTESY OF PHOTO COLLECTION, FORSYTH COUNTY PUBLIC LIBRARY.

after the school superintendent, Julius Tomlinson, had made trips to northern cities to raise money to supplement the special tax funds, which had been divided equally between the white school and the black school.

At the turn of the century, Winston still had no hospital to serve blacks, but R. J. Reynolds had offered to match up to $5,000 if money could be raised in the black community. When the time came he was as good as his word. Many of the people who were treated in both the white and the black hospitals worked for him, and he said later that he had helped get the Negro hospital built because it would help his sick employees get back to work.

Diseases which have long since been eradicated were an ever-present threat to life in the nineteenth century, and in Rondthaler's record the deaths of children are sadly enumerated each year.

Fire, too, was a danger never far from people's minds. The year 1892 was a particularly bad one for conflagrations. Fire destroyed six stores and damaged a bank building on Courthouse Square in November. A mill burned in a separate fire the same day. The big new Zinzendorf Hotel on Glade Street in the West End burned to the ground on Thanksgiving Day, ending a brief dream that Winston might become a resort town. At Christmas three new houses in the West End burned down. Salem's firefighters rushed to Winston's aid in these emergencies, and Rondthaler noted "the manner in which the hard-worked and faithful firemen have toiled together on so many occasions has been a sign that the two towns are really one."

But progress and prosperity were the dominant themes. Crowds cheered when Winston's new electric street lights were turned on in 1887, and for several evenings they continued to gather near the main switch to watch the magical illumination. A similar stir was created three years later when electric street cars were put into operation. Again a

Dr. Simon Green Atkins

❖

Simon Atkins was the founder of what is now Winston-Salem State University and the father of many other institutions that substantially improved the conditions and prospects of the black citizens of Forsyth County. He came to Winston in 1890 to be principal of the Depot Street Graded School, and died in Winston-Salem in 1934 at the end of a remarkable career.

Born to parents who had been slaves in Chatham County, he graduated with distinction from Saint Augustine's College in Raleigh and immediately became head of the grammar school department of Livingstone College in Salisbury. At this time he was a contributor to *The Southland,* a monthly publication that spoke for and to the blacks of the South. A year after arriving in Winston, he started the development of the Columbian Heights neighborhood (named for the Columbian Exposition in Chicago) as a way of promoting home ownership among black citizens. He and his wife, Oleona, were the first residents of the new neighborhood.

The Depot Street School was by then serving 1,000 students, but not providing them with the practical training that Dr. Atkins and other leaders in the black community believed they would need to make a living in the segregated South. Hoping to have Winston chosen as the site for a new state land grant college for blacks, Atkins and his group solicited the donation of 50 acres of land, and raised $2,000 in the black community and an additional $500 from R. J. Reynolds. The college went to Greensboro, but Atkins proceeded to start an industrial school without state support. Slater Industrial Academy opened in 1892 with money raised from both white and black people in the community.

With Atkins at its head, Slater eventually dropped the high school program and became a teachers' college. In 1925, as Winston-Salem Teachers College, it was the first black institution in the nation to offer a Bachelor of Science degree in elementary education.

In the late 1890s Dr. Atkins turned his attention to getting a hospital established in the same Columbian Heights district. Again he led the fund-raising efforts in the black and white communities, and Slater Hospital opened in 1902.

Simon Atkins was awarded an honorary Doctor of Laws degree from Howard University in 1928, and the citation read on that occasion sums up his contribution to the history of Winston-Salem: Teacher of youth; builder and sustainer of educational institutions; leader of cooperative activity in the teaching profession; responsible and trusted citizen; nucleus and maker of interracial goodwill.

RICHARD JOSHUA REYNOLDS FINALLY
MARRIED MARY KATHARINE SMITH
WHEN HE WAS 54 YEARS OLD. THEY
ARE SHOWN HERE WITH THEIR FOUR
CHILDREN. PHOTO COURTESY OF
REYNOLDA HOUSE MUSEUM OF
AMERICAN ART.

cheering crowd assembled, a Salem band played, and joy riders reveled in their new means of getting around.

On the eve of the twentieth century the Fries family's cotton mill, Arista Mills, was turning out 15,000 yards of cloth a day. The financial institution that would tower above the rest as its headquarters building dominates Winston-Salem's skyline today had been born, as Wachovia Loan & Trust Company, another of Francis H. Fries' endeavors. R. J. Reynolds had sharpened his sales and advertising tactics and was starting to absorb his competitors, even as the powerful American Tobacco monopoly was temporarily cramping his expansive style. A Brooklyn machinist named William Briggs had come to town. Backed by some of the tobacco leaders, he invented a machine that could turn out 300,000 cigarettes a day. The Nissen and Spach wagon works, both old firms, were profiting from the tobacco trade,

their horse-drawn carriages (called Nissens and Spachs the way we speak of Chevys or Toyotas today) transporting tobacco instead of settlers. Construction companies were building 100 houses a year.

Winston and Salem had grown to a community of about 30,000 people. When the post offices consolidated in 1899, the hyphen was stamped into official use. The new postmark reflected what the old Moravian town and the rough-and-tumble county seat had become, and were already called by the people who lived here— Winston-Salem. ❖

Bulding of the hotell
Zinzendorf
T.C. Enge

THE ZINZENDORF HOTEL ON GLADE STREET
BURNED TO THE GROUND ON THANKSGIVING DAY
OF 1892. THE FIRE ENDED A BRIEF DREAM THAT
WINSTON MIGHT BECOME A RESORT TOWN.
PHOTO COURTESY OF THE WACHOVIA HISTORICAL
SOCIETY.

Richard Joshua Reynolds

❖

By the time he had achieved legendary fame, R. J. Reynolds seemed to enjoy cultivating a "rags to riches" story about himself. He boasted of doing rugged manufacturing work as a seven-year-old child, claimed to have been promoted to superintendency of a factory at 18, and told reporters that he started as "an ordinary factory hireling." The workers in his factories believed him to be virtually illiterate, and RJR apparently didn't feel a need to correct that impression.

In fact, he was not poor or uneducated. He was one of 16 children born to Hardin and Nancy Cox Reynolds of Patrick County, Virginia. Among his extensive business operations, Hardin Reynolds grew, manufactured, and sold tobacco. He involved all his sons in the family business. Any back-breaking labor, such as RJR hinted at in later years, was done by slaves. Young R. J., known in the family as Dick, got his early schooling in Patrick County, completed two years at Emory and Henry College, and took business courses at a college in Baltimore. Math was the only subject at which he excelled. One of his brothers told a newspaper reporter many years later that RJR discovered, after his formal education was long behind him, that he had an "ocular defect" which made it very difficult for him to read. Although he was an indifferent student, no one ever seems to have doubted his intelligence. From childhood he showed himself to be quick to learn from experience, very adaptable, assertive, and independent-minded.

When he rode into Winston in 1874, R. J. Reynolds had experience in peddling tobacco in rural areas and of taking orders for chewing tobacco, which he had done in Baltimore. He also had $7,500 in cash in his pocket. At 24 he was a tall, robust man, and he cut a dashing figure in the little town of Winston. He was liked and respected by the other businessmen, and, as an eligible bachelor for 30 years, he honored several of his favorite girls by naming brands of his chewing tobacco for them.

When he finally married at the age of 54, he chose a distant cousin, Mary Katharine Smith. Family tradition has it that he had known her all her life, and teasingly told her when she was a child that he would marry her when she grew up. Before RJR died in 1918, they had four children.

Chapter 3

✦

Shaping the Twin City
(1900-1929)

MUCH OF WINSTON-SALEM'S POPULATION GROWTH
IN THE EARLY TWENTIETH CENTURY CAME FROM
THE INFLUX OF BLACK PEOPLE WHO CAME TO
WORK IN THE TOBACCO FACTORIES. SHOWN
HERE ARE STUDENTS AT FOURTEENTH STREET
SCHOOL CANING CHAIRS.

✦

PHOTO COURTESY OF SOCIETY FOR THE STUDY OF
AFRO-AMERICAN HISTORY IN FORSYTH COUNTY.

PLEASANT HENDERSON HANES, WITH
HIS TWO SONS WILL AND P. HUBER,
FOUNDED THE P. H. HANES KNITTING
COMPANY, WHICH ORIGINALLY PRODUCED
MEN'S TWO-PIECE UNDERWEAR. PHOTO
COURTESY OF PHOTO COLLECTION,
FORSYTH COUNTY PUBLIC LIBRARY.

In the first quarter of the twentieth century, Winston-Salem grew to be the largest and wealthiest city in North Carolina. The city's most expansive period began in the first decade with significant developments in two important industries, tobacco and textiles.

In 1901 the Hanes brothers, Pleasant and John Wesley, each started their own textile mills. The brothers had been very successful manufacturers of plug tobacco for a quarter century, but as the American Tobacco Company trust (of which R. J. Reynolds Tobacco was a subsidiary) grew in power, the Haneses were among the many companies that sold their interests to Reynolds and the trust. John Wesley Hanes' illness in 1899 may have also been a factor in the decision to sell. Though both brothers were in the their 50s, they turned to textiles rather than retiring on their very comfortable incomes.

John Wesley Hanes recovered from his illness, opened Shamrock Hosiery Mills on Marshall Street downtown, and began manufacturing men's and children's socks. The company grew rapidly, changed its name to Hanes Hosiery Mills Company, and by 1920 was making women's hosiery primarily. A unique company benefit was that employees were given new dry socks when they came to work on wet days. The factory building, with its distinctive "sawtooth" roofline that was installed to improve lighting and insulation, is one of Winston-Salem's enduring downtown landmarks and, since 1982, has been the home of arts organizations, gallery spaces, and a restaurant.

Pleasant Henderson Hanes, with his two sons Will and P. Huber, founded the P. H. Hanes Knitting Company, which originally produced men's two-piece underwear. In 1910 the company built its own yarn spinning plant west of town, on what is now busy Stratford Road. The company built 180 houses for employees around the plant, and Hanestown had its own school, police protection, churches, company store, baseball field, and volunteer fire department. The company took a paternalistic interest in the families of its workers, providing a nurse, planting acres of greens to improve their health, and ordering milk for children who were undernourished. Much later, in the 1950s, the company made the houses available for sale to employees, at bargain prices.

Although customers never made a distinction between Hanes hosiery and Hanes underwear, the two enterprises were separate until 1965, when they merged to become the Hanes Corporation and were listed on the New York Stock Exchange.

Meanwhile, R. J. Reynolds had sold controlling interest in his tobacco company to the American Tobacco trust and had been assigned to manufacturing plug tobacco. But he was looking to the day when the trust would be dissolved and preparing for entry into what he accurately foresaw would be the huge market—smoking tobacco. In 1907 he introduced Prince Albert smoking tobacco and, not put off by a threatened lawsuit by the trust, began an aggressive marketing campaign.

PRINCE ALBERT

-the national joy smoke

R. J. REYNOLDS INTRODUCED PRINCE ALBERT SMOKING TOBACCO IN 1907. CLEARLY A MARKETING GENIUS, HE NAMED THE BRAND AND CAME UP WITH MANY OF ITS ADVERTISING SLOGANS. PHOTO COURTESY OF R. J. REYNOLDS TOBACCO COMPANY.

Prince Albert became the leading brand of smoking tobacco within its first few years, and its success was a turning point in the company's history. It was the first brand to be nationally advertised, with ads created by an agency placed in *The Saturday Evening Post, Collier's Weekly*, and the other mass market magazines of the day, and a giant electrically lighted sign in New York City's Union Square promoting "The Nation's Joy Smoke." The company's production and packaging operations were challenged to keep up with the demand, as production expanded from 250,000 pounds annually to 14 million pounds by 1911.

Reynolds himself named the brand, came up with many of its advertising slogans, and conceived of the hermetically-sealed humidors in which it came to be sold. He was clearly a marketing genius, and in the early 1890s had proved to his own satisfaction the power of advertising, with billboards, posters, teaser ads in newspapers, bonuses, coupons, and special promotions. He kept a close hand on this side of the business, choosing gifted artists to create beautiful images for his ads and packages, dreaming up names that would capture the imagination of consumers, and personally approving all design and copy.

When the tobacco trust was dissolved by court order in 1911, Reynolds was ready to move into cigarette manufacturing. He intended to dominate that rapidly expanding market, and with Camels, introduced in 1913, he did. Reynolds is said to have spent $1.5 million in advertising for Camels in the first year. By the time of his death in 1918, Camels had captured 40 percent of the market. In 1921, the year the famous "I'd walk a mile for a Camel" slogan came into being, about half of all the 36 billion cigarettes Americans were smoking each year were Camels.

Reynolds and Hanes weren't solely responsible for Winston-Salem's nickname, "City of Industry." The venerable Arista Mills, which made cotton for work shirts, had been founded by Francis H. Fries. It continued and thrived under the leadership of his son-in-law, Agnew Bahnson. Chatham Mills moved to Winston from Elkin and sold blankets nationally. Indera Mills, another creation of Francis Fries (with his nephew W. LeDoux Siewers), made knee warmers and slips at first, and added rayon bloomers to the line during the 1920s. Another Fries nephew, Fred Bahnson, joined with his brother Agnew and their brother-in-law James A. Gray to sell a humidifier the Bahnsons had

FOR ENTERTAINMENT AND ENLIGHTENMENT, THE PEOPLE OF THE TOWN VISITED THE CARNEGIE LIBRARY ON CHERRY STREET. PHOTO COURTESY OF PHOTO COLLECTION, FORSYTH COUNTY PUBLIC LIBRARY.

GEORGE BLACK'S HANDIWORK IS
LITERALLY BUILT INTO THE HISTORY OF
WINSTON-SALEM. HIS HANDMADE BRICKS
BROUGHT HIM NATIONAL ACCLAIM. PHOTO
COURTESY OF PHOTO COLLECTION,
FORSYTH COUNTY PUBLIC LIBRARY.

designed for their Uncle Francis. Their business was eventually called The Bahnson Company, and its 1924 factory on South Marshall Street is now a small business incubator. The Douglas Battery company, still one of the city's leading businesses, got its start in 1918. The city's thriving wagon-making industry, was, of course, eventually sidelined by the automobile, and some of those companies became manufacturers of furniture. In the late 1920s, furniture making was the city's second largest industry.

The twentieth century brought not only manufacturing growth and wealth but also change and variety to daily life. Automobiles, telephones, and movies opened up new and exciting vistas. For entertainment and enlightenment, the people of the town could go to band concerts on Courthouse Square, to hear famous speakers and musicians at the 2,300-seat Elks Auditorium, to the Liberty or the Amuzu or several other movie palaces for a nickel, and to the new Carnegie Library on Cherry Street. Train excursions were popular, and the streetcar line went as far as Nissen Park, a large and now long-forgotten amusement park which had a zoo, bowling alley, movie pavilion, nature trails, and picnic areas.

Social life was enriched by the formation of clubs for virtually all ages, conditions, and interests. Women organized book clubs, music clubs, garden clubs, and purely social clubs. In the large black community, neighborhood clubs were a primary means of sharing information and raising support for a variety of improvement projects.

THE ASSOCIATED CHARITIES OF WINSTON MADE SUBSTANTIAL CONTRIBUTIONS TO THE QUALITY OF LIFE IN YOUNG WINSTON-SALEM. "MISS ANNIE" GROGAN, WHO SERVED AS SECRETARY OF THE ORGANIZATION, WAS A FAMILIAR SIGHT ON THE STREETS OF THE CITY, MAKING CHARITABLE CALLS IN HER HORSE-DRAWN BUGGY, AND LATER HER ROADSTER. SHE WAS KNOWN AS THE CITY'S "MOTHER OF CHARITY." PHOTO COURTESY OF PHOTO COLLECTION, FORSYTH COUNTY PUBLIC LIBRARY.

WITHIN THE BLACK COMMUNITY, SUCCESSFUL AND LASTING BUSINESS VENTURES WERE ESTABLISHED, INCLUDING THE SAFE BUS COMPANY. THE COMPANY WAS FOUNDED IN 1926 BY A GROUP OF PRIVATE BUS DRIVERS, UNDER THE LEADERSHIP OF C. T. WOODLAND. IT IS BELIEVED TO HAVE BEEN THE LARGEST BLACK-OWNED TRANSPORTATION SYSTEM IN THE WORLD UNTIL 1972, WHEN IT WAS PURCHASED BY THE CITY AND BECAME PART OF THE WINSTON-SALEM TRANSIT AUTHORITY. PHOTO COURTESY OF PHOTO COLLECTION, FORSYTH COUNTY PUBLIC LIBRARY.

The Winston-Salem Automobile Club was one of the first in the South, at a time when horse-drawn carriages, street-cars, and feet were still the prevalent means of conveyance. Businessmen gathered at the Twin City Club, at the corner of Fourth and Marshall Streets, to talk about news and politics, and at Forsyth Country Club, founded in 1913, to play golf. The town also had a polo club, and one of the top-ranked teams in the South. Following the pattern of the rest of the country, civic clubs took hold in the second decade of the century, beginning with Rotary in 1915. Kiwanis, Business and Professional Women's Club, Lions, Civitan, and Altrusa soon followed.

The "Y" movement was at its height in the early years of the century, and a major event of 1906 was the whirlwind campaign to raise money for a new YMCA building at the corner of Fourth and Cherry Streets. The success of the campaign was signaled by the clanging of the fire alarm on the evening of December 7—one ring for each $1,000

of the $55,000 raised by public sub-scription. The building opened in 1908, and in the same year a YWCA was started in the Presbyterian Church, mostly as a service for young working women who lived in boardinghouses and needed a place to get together and relax in their free time.

Clubs and Y's and many societal structures segregated the sexes in this period, and women were not yet active in political life. On the subject of suf-frage, Bishop Rondthaler wrote in the Home Moravian Church Memorabilia of 1911: "Shall women vote? They are thinking quietly about it, and when they have made up their minds the result will be according to their best and widest thought. Men will never say nay to what the mother, the wife, the sister, the friend clearly sees to be for the best interest of the human society of which she is the very life and crown."

But woman's place was not only on a pedestal. Two women's organizations which made substantial contributions to the quality of life in young

George Black

❖

George Black's handiwork is literally built into the history of Winston-Salem. His handmade bricks have been used in the restoration of Old Salem, more than a dozen banks, and some of the city's finest houses. He came to Winston in 1889 from Liberty, North Carolina, with his father and brother. Months later, George's father died, and the 10-year-old boy found work in a white-owned brickmaking company. He learned the craft well and later began making bricks on his own to sell. During the 1920s, Black joined with another skilled brickmaker and opened a brickyard. As interest in traditional crafts grew, Black was called upon by Colonial Williamsburg, and his work was featured on a national television program. In his 90s, he went to Guyana to teach brickmaking under the auspices of the United States Agency for International Development. He was entertained in Washington by President Nixon upon his return, and he was later presented with the Freedom Foundation's George Washington Medal of Honor for his humanitarian mission.

CIVIC PRIDE BROUGHT WITH IT THE DESIRE TO HAVE WINSTON-SALEM LOOK LIKE THE PROSPEROUS, PROGRESSIVE PLACE IT WAS. TROLLEY CARS BECAME AS FAMILIAR A SIGHT ON CITY STREETS AS THE LOCALLY-MADE WAGONS. PHOTO COURTESY OF PHOTO COLLECTION, FORSYTH COUNTY PUBLIC LIBRARY.

Winston-Salem were the Associated Charities of Winston and the Women's Improvement League. Associated Charities was organized in 1905, following the bursting of the city's reservoir in November of 1904. In Winston's worst disaster, 180,000 gallons of water coursed through the streets, demolishing eight houses, killing nine people, and injuring many more. The Associated Charities provided an organized way of helping victims of future tragedies and disasters. These women raised money and donations of merchandise through door-to-door canvassing, and used it to ameliorate some of the worst social problems of the day, the tragedies that resulted from unemployment, child labor, racial segregation, and tuberculosis. This organization was active until 1940, when its functions were absorbed by the Welfare Department.

During these same years it was women who made the effort to keep Winston's streets, school yards, and public buildings clean and safe. Through the Women's Improvement League they successfully campaigned for regular street cleaning, metal garbage cans, and enforcement of laws to keep the sidewalks, the post office, and the railway station from becoming giant cuspidors.

The segregation of the sexes was, of course, trivial in comparison with the segregation of the black and white races. Much of Winston-Salem's population growth in the early twentieth century came from the influx of black people who came to work in the tobacco factories, many from rural South Carolina. It is estimated that the black population grew from about 5,000 in 1890 to more than 20,000 in 1920, and some 60 percent worked in the tobacco industry. Since most public facilities and services were closed to them, black people established their own institutions parallel to the white institutions. The growth and prosperity of the city was reflected in the black community, which was extremely unusual in the South for its high concentration of educated professional and business people, and home ownership in attractive, well-built, comfortable neighborhoods.

In this growing and thriving period, the black community had its own doctors, dentists, lawyers, real estate companies, tailors, shoemakers, dressmakers, and barbers. Blacks owned and operated more than a hundred neighborhood groceries, several drugstores, four theaters, and a number of dance halls, night clubs, and billiard rooms. Black professionals had their offices in black-owned office buildings, including the Atlantic, the Bruce, the Charles Jones, the Ogburn, and the Lincoln Theatre.

The black community was in every sense a community. Within it, successful and lasting business ventures were established, including the Safe Bus Company, Winston Mutual Insurance Company, and Forsyth Bank. A branch of the YWCA was established by and for black women. The black community had its own baseball league and its own agricultural fair. Local units of the International Tobacco Workers Union helped black laborers to better their often miserable working conditions. Fraternal and civic organizations and local chapters of fraternities and sororities flourished. The black community organized its own volunteer fire departments.

Excluded by the white population, black people in Winston-Salem created their own supportive and cohesive city within the city. It produced outstanding leaders in the fields of business, education, medicine, and the church, and older residents of Winston-Salem today recall the 1920s and '30s as a time of strong neighborhoods and shared values. What bound this segment of the population together was a belief that patience, education, and hard work would ultimately lead to legal and social equality.

Civic pride brought with it the desire to have Winston-Salem look like the prosperous, progressive place it was. In 1913, the year Winston and Salem were formally merged, the Retail Merchants Association created a downtown "white way"—a paved, electrically lighted thoroughfare along West Fourth Street from Liberty Street to Grace Park. The project initially met with objections— the dazzling illumination was expected to work a hardship on people who lived in the area—but it was such a success in drawing both local citizens and outsiders that it led to more paved and lighted streets.

Putting the Camel into Camel City

❖

The year 1913 is significant not only for the consolidation of Winston and Salem but also for the birth of the brand that captured the burgeoning cigarette market. Camel was one of four brands R. J. Reynolds developed and test-marketed that year, at a time when most cigarette smokers still rolled their own.

Old Joe, the animal pictured on the cigarette pack, was a controversial character in advertising campaigns of the 1990s, but in 1913 he was a dromedary in the Barnum and Bailey Circus. When the circus came to Winston-Salem in September of that year, the tobacco company hadn't come up with a good camel illustration for its new cigarette packs. Roy C. Haberkern, secretary to R. J. Reynolds, took a photographer over to the circus to search for a suitable symbol.

He found the creature he had in mind, but getting its image on film proved to be difficult. First, the menagerie keeper wouldn't cooperate (Haberkern forged Reynolds' signature on a release to allow the photography), and then the dromedary wouldn't stand still to have his picture taken. The trainer slapped him on the nose, and the camera recorded Old Joe's indignant reaction—tail raised, ears back, eyes shut. The contrary dromedary is one of the best-known advertising symbols in the world—and is responsible for the fairly common misconception that camels have only one hump.

Katharine Smith Reynolds

✥

Her life was short, but her influence on the development of Winston-Salem was enduring. Before she was his wife, Kate Smith was Richard Joshua Reynolds' employee. She went to work as his secretary after graduating from college and briefly teaching art in her hometown of Mount Airy. Though she was 30 years younger than her rich and influential husband, Katharine was well-suited by her forceful character, her intelligence, and her commitment to public service to make the most of the scope and advantages that marriage brought to her. She was the main force behind the development of Reynolda House and Village, and her interests ranged far beyond fashions, flowers, and furnishings. She organized model schools for white and black children on the estate and evening literacy classes for adults. Concerned about working conditions in the factories, she encouraged her husband to provide medical services and cafeterias for employees and a nursery for children of women workers. She was active in a wide array of social causes at the local, state, and national levels, and was instrumental in organizing both the YWCA and the Junior League in Winston-Salem. A few years after Reynolds' death in 1918, she married J. Edward Johnston, who had been the principal of the school in Reynolda Village. She made generous endowments to colleges in the state and provided money for building both Old Town School and Reynolds High School. As a memorial to her first husband, she donated money to build Reynolds Auditorium, for decades the city's premier performance place. The building was completed shortly before her death on May 23, 1924. The community mourned her at a public memorial service at the auditorium, and by resolution of the Board of Aldermen, businesses throughout the city closed that afternoon in her honor.

The private fortunes that were being accumulated found their early expression in the building of large, handsome houses. At the turn of the century, the most fashionable residential neighborhoods were downtown, West End, and Washington Park. The city's leading industrialists lived on millionaires' rows on North Cherry Street and West Fifth Street in Winston and on the main streets of Salem. Both John Wesley Hanes and P. H. Hanes built houses on North Cherry Street. R. J. Reynolds, when he finally decided to stop living in a hotel room, built a house on Fifth Street in 1895. The institution of street-car lines in the 1890s led to the development of both West End and Washington Park. West End, a hilly neighborhood of curving streets, was laid out by Jacob Lott Ludlow, the city's first engineer. It was the first purely residential neighborhood—most of the city houses and tenements were interspersed among business and factories—but it was quickly followed by the development of suburbs.

R. J. Reynolds himself led the move to the suburbs with the building of his magnificent estate, Reynolda. Reynolds and his young wife, Katharine, gradually bought more than a thousand acres of land west of the city and hired Charles Barton Keen, a Philadelphia architect, to design their country house, and Thomas W. Sears, a Philadelphia landscape architect, to lay out the gardens and grounds. The 60-room country house, known as The Bungalow, was sustained by barns, a blacksmith shop, a chapel, a school, and a post office, all built to match in a green-roofed Dutch colonial style. Reynolda Village, as it was called, was completed in 1917 and employed a staff of more than a hundred people.

Reynolda House, now a museum of American art, is one of Winston-Salem's foremost architectural, historical, and cultural treasures. It is also the setting for the city's most famous mystery, the death of young Zachary Smith Reynolds in 1932. Reynolda

Gardens today is a beauty spot cherished by city residents and a regular stop for tourists. Reynolda Village is an elegant shopping area, the old service buildings converted to specialty shops, galleries, restaurants, and professional offices. Much of the remainder of the Reynolda estate is now the campus of Wake Forest University.

Reynolds also took an interest in the living conditions of his employees. Before his death, when some 10,000 people were working in his tobacco factories, he set in motion a plan for the company to build houses and sell them to employees at reasonable costs. Both black and white neighborhoods were built for employees.

In 1921 William N. Reynolds, who operated the business after R. J.'s death, followed his brother's example and bought a 1,000-acre estate near Clemmons. He enlarged the antebellum manor house on the property and planted orchards and gardens. In his will Reynolds left Tanglewood to the people of Forsyth County, and the huge park is a favorite picnic, camping, and recreation area. Today it is home of the annual Steeplechase Races, the North Carolina Chili Championship, and the summer Music at Sunset concerts of the Winston-Salem Piedmont Triad Symphony. In recent years Tanglewood has added a winter attraction, a Festival of Lights during the Christmas season.

Nobody else's "bungalows" matched those of the Reynolds brothers, but many stately mansions were built in the teens and twenties, primarily in Reynolda Park, Buena Vista (which in Winston-Salem is pronounced *Byoo-na Vista*), West Highlands, and Country Club Estates. Many of the wealthiest families left downtown and West End for these western suburbs, which have aged gracefully and retained their residential character. This abundance of architecturally distinctive houses on large, well-landscaped lots is a striking feature of Winston-Salem today.

The first suburb, however, was not a preserve of the wealthy. Ardmore, named for a Philadelphia suburb, began to be developed in 1914 in response to a rapidly growing need for more middle-class housing. For 22 years, houses were built in Ardmore at the rate of one per week, and with them came churches, a school, and a post office. In the past decade, Ardmore's charm has been discovered by a new generation of young families.

These older neighborhoods, both the grand and the modest, the black and the white, exhibit the full range of domestic building styles that prevailed in the years up until World War II and vibrantly preserve Winston-Salem's history. As this century draws to an end, the city's old housing stock is perhaps more valued than it has been since it was brand new. Bishop Rondthaler, in the Memorabilia of 1919, wrote, "The owning of homes by rich and poor, white and colored people, has given our citizenship the stability which is recognized far and near as a marked feature of Winston-Salem." Or in 1924: "Anybody who rides over the city of Winston-Salem, after having noted its increase in stately buildings, in greater or smaller churches, in school buildings, and in magnificent mansions, will come to the conclusion that, after all, its chief wealth is in the very great number of modest comfortable homes that have been built or are now in the process of building."

While most of the suburbs developed to the west of downtown, in the 1920s Montview, Forest Hills, Whiteview, and Bon Air were developed on the north side, and Konnoak Hills and Anderleigh were developed on the south side. While the older black neighborhoods of Columbian Heights and Boston continued, the

AT 22 STORIES, THE REYNOLDS TOBACCO HEADQUARTERS BUILDING WAS THE TALLEST BUILDING IN NORTH CAROLINA UNTIL THE 1950S. PHOTO COURTESY OF PHOTO COLLECTION, FORSYTH COUNTY PUBLIC LIBRARY.

Fourteenth Street and Alta Vista suburbs came into being. Throughout the decade, the city limits were expanded several times to take in the suburban developments.

As the city was spreading out, the downtown was shooting up. "Skyscraper" was a new word, and at the time of the consolidation of Winston and Salem, the Wachovia Bank Building, with seven stories, was the tallest building. It was followed by the 8-floor O'Hanlon Building in 1915, the 12-floor Hotel Robert E. Lee in 1921, the 18-floor Nissen Building in 1926, and the Carolina Theatre and Hotel building—now the Roger L. Stevens Center for the Performing Arts.

The grandest and tallest of the skyscrapers came in 1929. The Reynolds Tobacco headquarters building was designed by the New York architecture firm of Shreve & Lamb, who were told not to do anything flashy. The exterior is conservatively attractive; the interior is lavishly appointed with gold-leafed ceilings in the lobby, and many kinds of marble and beautiful wood panelling throughout. At 22 stories, it was the tallest building in North Carolina until the 1950s. Shreve & Lamb won the annual award of the National Association of Architects for its design, which led to a contract to design New York's Empire State Building. There's a clear resemblance between the two skyscrapers, which was recognized in a card received in Winston-Salem on the 50th anniversary of the Reynolds Building. It came from the Empire State Building, and it said, "Happy Birthday, Dad!"

The greater downtown area was also the site of most of the impressive church buildings constructed in the 1920s, including First Baptist, First Presbyterian, Augsburg Lutheran, Centenary United Methodist, and St. Paul's Episcopal. Other important and architecturally distinguished buildings of this period which survive are the old classical revival style post office (no longer in use), Reynolds Auditorium, and the colonial style *Winston-Salem Journal* building.

Concern for public health became organized and institutionalized, and both Winston-Salem and Forsyth County established health departments during the teens. Tuberculosis was the most serious and pervasive public health problem, and it would not be until after World War II that effective drug treatment would come into use. The worldwide influenza epidemic of 1918 hit Winston-Salem with a vengeance.

More than 10,000 cases were reported in Forsyth County during a six-week period that fall. Temporary hospitals were set up, including one with 50 beds in the J. W. Hanes home in the West End, and another at the Depot Street School. Temporary hospitals were again called into being in subsequent waves of the flu in 1919 and 1920, with prosperous black and white citizens offering their own houses for this purpose.

The Municipal Hospital, which opened in 1914, served both black and white patients. After it was enlarged, beginning in 1922 with a large bequest made by R. J. Reynolds on his deathbed, it became known as City Memorial Hospital. With several more additions, it would serve as Winston-Salem's main hospital for many decades, and for its whole existence City Memorial had its own nursing school.

Another hospital came into being at the same time City Memorial was undergoing its first expansion. Winston-Salem had made a successful bid to be the site of a regional hospital planned by the North Carolina Baptist Convention. Land was donated in what was called "the wilds of Ardmore," and over the protests of neighborhood residents, North Carolina Baptist Hospital was built and opened in 1923. With 88 beds, and the addition of a nursing school building, Baptist struggled for survival until the end of the Great Depression. In Winston-Salem's boom years, Baptist's day had not yet come, but it was to have a brilliant blossoming in the decades that followed.

As the Roaring Twenties drew to a close, Winston-Salem was home to the world's biggest manufacturer of tobacco products, the country's largest manufacturer of men's underwear, and the South's leading producers of knit and woolen goods and wagons. A quarter of all the products manufactured in North Carolina were made in Winston-Salem.

In the summer of 1929, Colonel Francis H. Fries, the president of Wachovia Bank and Trust Company,

AFTER MUNICIPAL HOSPITAL WAS ENLARGED, BEGINNING IN 1922 WITH A LARGE BEQUEST MADE BY R. J. REYNOLDS ON HIS DEATHBED, IT BECAME KNOWN AS CITY MEMORIAL HOSPITAL. PHOTO COURTESY OF PHOTO COLLECTION, FORSYTH COUNTY PUBLIC LIBRARY.

warned his fellow Rotarians to stop playing the stock market. He told them that a crash was inevitable, a prediction that was ridiculed in a newspaper editorial.

When the crash came in October, the exuberant expansion ended, but Winston-Salem was positioned to weather fairly well the lean years ahead. ❖

Chapter 4

✛

Company Town in Depression & War Years

(1930-1945)

SMITH REYNOLDS AIRPORT BECAME AN
IMPORTANT BASE FOR MILITARY TRAINING
DURING WORLD WAR II. HEAVY USE OF THE
AIRPORT BY THE UNITED STATES ARMY
AIR CORPS AND OTHER DEFENSE TRAFFIC
NECESSITATED MAJOR EXPANSION OF THE
NEW FACILITY. BY 1945 THE GOVERNMENT
HAD PUT $1,000,000 INTO IMPROVEMENTS
TO THE AIRPORT.

✛

PHOTO COURTESY OF PHOTO COLLECTION,
FORSYTH COUNTY PUBLIC LIBRARY.

BEGUN IN 1928, GRAYLYN, A STONE NORMAN REVIVAL STRUCTURE, WAS NOT COMPLETED UNTIL 1932. CONSTRUCTION WAS DELAYED BY PROTESTS OVER SUCH A CONSPICUOUS DISPLAY OF WEALTH AT A TIME WHEN MANY PEOPLE IN WINSTON-SALEM WERE SUFFERING. PHOTO COURTESY OF PHOTO COLLECTION, FORSYTH COUNTY PUBLIC LIBRARY.

*W*hen the Great Depression began, another of Winston-Salem's opulent mansions was under construction. Like Reynolda, the magnificent estate of Richard Joshua Reynolds, and Tanglewood, the country home of the brother who took over the business after Reynolds' death, Graylyn was being built by the president of Reynolds Tobacco Company. He was Bowman Gray, who had been an early protégé of Richard Joshua Reynolds.

Begun in 1928, Graylyn, a stone Norman Revival structure of which Luther Lashmit was the chief architect, was not completed until 1932. Construction was delayed by protests over such a conspicuous display of wealth at a time when many people in Winston-Salem were suffering.

But it was the wealth of people like Bowman Gray and the prosperity of companies like Reynolds Tobacco that spared Winston-Salem from the worst effects of the Depression. This city fared better in that decade than did many other places in America.

At the depth of the Depression, some 10,000 people in the city of 75,000 were subsisting entirely on public relief. None of the city's major companies went under, though all did some retrenching. Hanes Knitting Company stopped production of rayon goods, and Reynolds Tobacco shortened its work week, but didn't lay workers off.

The thousands of people who worked in the city's factories continued to benefit from the benevolent paternalism that had been established early in the century. Reynolds employees had long enjoyed company-provided medical care and stock ownership. In the early 1930s, 800,000 shares of the company's Class A stock were owned by employees. In Hanestown, rents were low— 50 cents per week per room in 1938, including electricity and water—and residents also had medical care and other company benefits.

Private efforts helped improve the lot of the unemployed. The Rotary Club quietly worked out an arrangement with the city to pay for the school lunches of those who couldn't afford the 25-cent cost, and to keep municipal parks and playgrounds open in the summer.

The Depression caused Winston-Salem's business leaders to consider, for the first time, the desirability of recruiting businesses from outside. Until then, the city's industrialists had preferred the homegrown, and had managed by and large to keep unions out and to maintain the loyalty of employees by their paternalistic largesse. But in 1930 they established an Industrial Commission to boost the local economy by attracting outside companies. The effort came to nothing, since almost no companies were seeking to expand or relocate at the time, but the list of favorable attributes the commission drew up are telling. Besides the good climate, transportation, and excellent record of industrial growth, North Carolina had to offer no minimum wage, laws that allowed 60-hour work weeks, legal employment of children as young as 14, and 11-hour work days for women and children.

The men who ran the companies also ran local government, and a certain insensitivity to how the other half lived is also evident in a decision of the Board of Aldermen in 1935. The United States Congress had voted money for public housing, but the city fathers were having none of it. They officially declared that Winston-Salem had no slums—at a time when some of its citizens were living over open sewage, and one 32-unit tenement block was served by a single cold water tap and three outdoor privies. This attitude was later reversed when Richard J. Reynolds Jr. ran for mayor in 1941 on a platform that included slum clearance and public housing. After he was elected, the city was granted authority to build more than

300 units, a project which had to wait until several years after the end of World War II.

The established colleges survived the Depression. Winston-Salem Teachers College, formerly Slater Normal School, was operating under state control as a four-year college for black students, and Salem College and Academy, the oldest educational institution in the city, was thriving with enrollments of about 600 young women. Three new high schools came into being in the first years of the decade: Hanes High School, Gray High School, and Atkins High School.

It was a bleak day for public education when the state took over full responsibility for financing it. Teachers' salaries and school terms were cut, and classrooms had as many as 50 pupils. Music, art, and physical education were

THE WEALTH OF PEOPLE LIKE BOWMAN GRAY JR. AND DICK REYNOLDS, AND THE PROSPERITY OF COMPANIES LIKE REYNOLDS TOBACCO, SPARED WINSTON-SALEM FROM THE WORST EFFECTS OF THE DEPRESSION. THIS CITY FARED BETTER IN THAT DECADE THAN DID MANY OTHER PLACES IN AMERICA. PHOTO COURTESY OF PHOTO COLLECTION, FORSYTH COUNTY PUBLIC LIBRARY.

THE TWIN CITY HEARD ITS FIRST RADIO BROADCASTS IN
1930. WSJS BEGAN BROADCASTING ON GOOD FRIDAY OF
THAT YEAR, WITH A RELIGIOUS PROGRAM FEATURING THE
MORAVIAN BISHOP RONDTHALER AND THE ST. PAUL'S
EPISCOPAL CHURCH CHOIR. PHOTO COURTESY OF PHOTO
COLLECTION, FORSYTH COUNTY PUBLIC LIBRARY.

all but eliminated from the curriculum.
Forsyth County citizens didn't put up
with these hardships for long. They
voted themselves a tax to supplement
the state support of the schools, but,
meanwhile, one of the city's most illus-
trious private schools came into being
because of parents' concerns about the
poverty-stricken curriculum and over-
crowded classrooms. Summit School
opened in 1933 with 18 students in a
private house in the West End.

The Twin City heard its first radio
broadcasts in 1930. WSJS got its call
letters from its owner, the *Winston-
Salem Journal and Sentinel,* and it operated out of the newspaper building on
North Marshall Street. Broadcasting
began on Good Friday of that year, with

a religious program featuring the
Moravian Bishop Rondthaler and the
St. Paul's Episcopal Church choir. The
Moravian Easter sunrise service was
broadcast that weekend for the first
time. In recent years WSJS has had
an all-talk format, but at first it was
almost all music, with live performances
by the 16-piece WSJS Orchestra, the
Winston-Salem Harmonica Band, and
a novelty act with a musical saw,
among others. By 1937 a second radio
station, WAIR, was broadcasting
from the city's foremost hotel, the
Robert E. Lee.

Also organized in the '30s were
music associations, of which the Mozart
Club may be the sole survivor. Its annual presentation of Handel's *Messiah*

still packs Reynolds Auditorium the first Sunday in December.

Horses and streetcars disappeared from the streets, giving way to buses, taxis, and private automobiles. The trolleys stopped running in 1936, and the last hitching posts were soon removed from downtown streets, to be replaced by parking meters.

About the same time, Winston-Salem's airport was being improved and expanded, with a large infusion of Reynolds money. In 1942, shortly before Mayor Dick Reynolds left for naval duty in the war, the airport was named for his late brother, Smith Reynolds.

Reynolds money also had a big hand in building the city's long-awaited hospital for blacks, and its biggest municipal park. William and Kate Reynolds provided money for Kate Bitting Reynolds Memorial Hospital, which opened in 1938. Richard J. Reynolds Jr. was the benefactor of Reynolds Park, which opened in 1940 with roller skating rinks, outdoor bowling lanes, and a permanent carnival.

Bowman Gray, whose elaborate house had caused such controversy in 1930, died in 1935. His sons continued to be key members of Winston-Salem's leadership; Bowman Gray Jr. would become president of Reynolds Tobacco, and his brother Gordon would become owner of the city's newspapers, a radio station, and later a television station. The family fortune, like those of Reynolds and Hanes, began changing the face and future of the city soon after Bowman Gray Sr.'s death.

Bowman Gray Memorial Stadium was dedicated in 1939, having been built under the Work Projects Administration with matching funds from the Gray family.

Two years later the medical school of Wake Forest College in Wake Forest, North Carolina, was persuaded to move to Winston-Salem with gifts from the same family. Named the Bowman Gray School of Medicine, it was located next to North Carolina Baptist Hospital on Hawthorne Road, and the coordinated efforts of the hospital and the medical school combined to create a great regional medical center, one of Winston-Salem's healthiest enterprises and largest employers today.

War threw the factories into overtime. The Hanes operations made 38 million garments for the armed forces, and Reynolds factories churned out billions of Camels for servicemen. More than 13,000 men and women from the

AS A MEMORIAL TO HER FIRST HUSBAND, KATHARINE REYNOLDS DONATED THE MONEY TO BUILD REYNOLDS AUDITORIUM. PHOTO COURTESY OF PHOTO COLLECTION, FORSYTH COUNTY PUBLIC LIBRARY.

Those Daring Young Men in Their Flying Machines

❖

On an October day in 1927, a huge crowd gathered in Hanes Park to cheer the young man who was America's hero and darling that year—Charles Lindbergh. He was on his way to dedicate Winston-Salem's new Miller Municipal Airport. He circled low over the park to give everyone a good look at the *Spirit of Saint Louis*, in which he had made the world's first solo transatlantic flight just months before. Later in the day, the crowd tore up the chair he had sat on for its splinter souvenirs.

One of Winston-Salem's most enthusiastic flyboys was Zachary Smith Reynolds, son of R. J. Reynolds. In 1927, at age 16, he was one of the youngest pilots in the country. Flying was so new that licensing was not required, but Smith Reynolds had chosen to be tested and certified by Orville Wright, and he had his license. A year or so later, when the federal government instituted licensing, he was immediately granted a transport license that allowed him to fly commercially. In 1931 he made a 17,000 mile flight from England to China in an 80-horsepower amphibian. He was dead at 21, killed by a gun at the Reynolda estate after a party one summer night in 1932. He is remembered in the Z. Smith Reynolds Foundation established by his brother and sisters, a grant from which expanded, improved, and renamed Miller Airport.

On his visit Lindbergh had challenged Winston-Salem to take the lead in aviation in North Carolina. In the crowd that day was a 9-year-old boy who would take up that challenge. Tom Davis learned to fly at age 16, and at 20 he founded Piedmont Aviation, which played its part in the war by operating two pilot training schools. After the war was over, Davis' company began operating as Piedmont Airlines. Its phenomenal growth and excellent reputation were a source of pride to Piedmont's hometown.

county joined the military services, and those left at home faced shortages and rationing. As elsewhere, women took the jobs of men for the duration. Even children helped with the war effort, collecting tin cans and cigarette packaging foil, rolling bandages, and knitting scarves and mittens for the troops.

After a decade with few business start-ups, Winston-Salem got an important new industry in the war years. R. Y. Sharpe established Pilot Freight Carriers in 1941. Two years later, Malcom McLean moved his McLean Trucking Company to Winston-Salem, and the city was on its way to becoming an important trucking center.

Fifteen years of depression and war had left Winston-Salem with its power structure intact. Not only its large industries, but also its civic affairs were in the hands of a small number of families, most prominently the Reynolds, Hanes, Grays, and Fries. The children and grandchildren of the founders of the companies built on what had been handed down to them and made the somewhat unusual choice of keeping their company headquarters and manufacturing operations at home in Winston-Salem. Philanthropists on a grand scale, they endowed their hometown with schools and parks and medical facilities. Visionary, they invested in projects they knew would be important down the road—a first-class airport, a medical school, the communications industry.

Their wealth and their intense community involvement, their foresight and also their blindness, still gave Winston-Salem its shape and focus at the end of World War II. But the city where "everyone was either working on his second million or the second shift" was on the brink of change. ❖

TOM DAVIS LEARNED TO FLY AFTER HEARING CHARLES LINDBERGH'S DEDICATORY SPEECH AT MILLER MUNICIPAL AIRPORT. AT THE AGE OF 20, DAVIS FOUNDED PIEDMONT AVIATION. SHOWN HERE IS THE COMPANY'S FIRST GROUP OF PILOTS. PHOTO COURTESY OF PHOTO COLLECTION, FORSYTH COUNTY PUBLIC LIBRARY.

BOWMAN GRAY MEMORIAL STADIUM WAS DEDICATED IN 1939, HAVING BEEN BUILT UNDER THE WORK PROJECTS ADMINISTRATION WITH MATCHING FUNDS FROM THE GRAY FAMILY. SATURDAY NIGHT STOCK CAR RACES HAVE BEEN A POPULAR USE OF THE STADIUM, AND SOME OF NASCAR'S MOST FAMOUS DRIVERS GOT THEIR EARLY EXPERIENCE ON THE TRACK AT BOWMAN GRAY STADIUM. PHOTO COURTESY OF PHOTO COLLECTION, FORSYTH COUNTY PUBLIC LIBRARY.

Chapter 5

Community Improvement & Cultural Rebirth
(1946-1960)

THE FIRST MEETING OF THE CITY-
COUNTY PLANNING COMMISSION WAS
HELD MARCH 1948. THOSE IN
ATTENDANCE WERE (LEANING ON
TABLE) RUSSELL VAN NEST BLACK,
(LEFT TO RIGHT) MAYOR GEORGE
LENTZ, R. L. DIXON, CHARLES
NORFLEET, NAT CREWS, L. S.
O'GWYNN, ERIC GRUBB, KENNETH
GREENFIELD, R. B. BROWN, CHARLES
BABCOCK, T. E. JOHNSON,
G. CLAYTON HILL, R. A. THOMAS,
J. ERNEST YARBROUGH,
AND W. K. HOYT.

✤

PHOTO COURTESY OF PHOTO
COLLECTION, FORSYTH COUNTY
PUBLIC LIBRARY.

In the years following World War II, Winston-Salem's cooperative spirit came into full flower. The 100th anniversary of Forsyth County was on the horizon, and the county seat was taking stock of where it had come from and where it was headed. Plans and visions that had been sidelined by depression and war were taken up with renewed vigor.

One of those was the restoration of the old town of Salem. The visitors who walk through the serene streets of Old Salem today might well imagine that the Moravian town has retained its character and beauty continuously from the eighteenth century. In fact, the main street of Salem in the 1940s was in most ways just another busy thoroughfare, lined with nondescript business establishments and clogged with traffic. While many of the original buildings remained, they were used and altered as their owners chose, unencumbered by regulations and restrictions. All around the edges of the old settlement, land was being cleared for commercial development.

Through the years, a number of individuals had bought some of the houses and significant buildings of Salem to keep them safe from the bulldozer, but most citizens didn't seem to have given much thought to preserving the distinctive beginnings of their city. A writer of a letter to the editor of the newspaper claimed that the only significance of Old Salem was that George Washington had once slept there. Arthur Spaugh, a young industrialist and a lay leader of Home Moravian Church, and his wife Mary were among those who thought otherwise. They began dreaming about a large-scale restoration of Salem in 1938, after visiting Colonial Williamsburg.

THE MAIN STREET OF SALEM IN THE 1940S WAS IN MOST WAYS JUST ANOTHER BUSY THOROUGHFARE, LINED WITH BUSINESS ESTABLISHMENTS AND CLOGGED WITH TRAFFIC. AFTER RESTORATION EFFORTS, OLD SALEM BECAME THE EPITOME OF WINSTON-SALEM HOSPITALITY. SOME 300,000 PEOPLE VISIT EACH YEAR, INCLUDING HUNDREDS OF GROUPS OF SCHOOL CHILDREN. PHOTOS COURTESY OF PHOTO COLLECTION, FORSYTH COUNTY PUBLIC LIBRARY.

It would take a clash of post-war planning enthusiasm with post-war building activity to give impetus to that dream. Backed by the Chamber of Commerce, the city was moving toward creating a combined city-county planning commission and hiring a consultant to make recommendations on future development, including a new zoning ordinance. The *Winston-Salem Journal and Sentinel* ran a series of articles on planning, including the goal of preserving not only the ideals and traditions of the community, but also its historic landmarks. Meanwhile, building materials which had been scarce during the war years were again available, and the city building superintendent's office was swamped with applications for construc-

tion projects. Inevitably, perhaps, one of these projects threatened a historic property in Salem. An independent grocer proposed to build a new store on the site of the fifth house built in the Moravian town. Neighboring property owners fired off a petition to the Board of Aldermen to block the project, and from then on, preservation of Salem was on the public agenda.

Restoring Old Salem has been a monumental undertaking, which continues to this day. When the project began, about half of the buildings which had stood on 70 lots in 1820 were still there, most of them privately owned, and interspersed with more modern structures. Almost all had been extensively altered over the years, and clapboard siding, gables,

porches, and second stories masked their original character. The dwellings and shops of the early Moravians were surrounded by the necessary clutter of mid-twentieth-century municipal life—incongruous concrete sidewalks, paved roads, streetlights, stop signs, glaring yellow fire hydrants, and a maze of electrical and telephone wires and television antennas.

It's no wonder that many people couldn't see what was there to preserve, but in fact Salem had more to save and less to reconstruct than almost any historic district in the country. Furthermore, the meticulous records of the Moravians contained abundant evidence of how the early buildings looked and what each had been used for.

Old Salem Inc., a nonprofit corporation organized in 1950 with James A. Gray Jr. as its first president, began acquiring each property as it became available, and authentically restoring each building to a date in its history between 1766 and about 1840. Buildings that didn't belong to that period were gradually razed, and some buildings that had existed earlier were reconstructed from detailed plans in the Moravian archives.

The restoration could not have been accomplished without continuing support and cooperation of the community. The City of Winston-Salem, the Chamber of Commerce, the Retail Merchants Association, the Moravian Church, and Salem College and Academy were strong proponents in the crucial early stages. Most of the millions of dollars needed to preserve Old Salem have come from people who live in Winston-Salem, contributed in a series of capital campaigns led by prominent and concerned community leaders and supported by generous grants from local philanthropic foundations.

With more than 90 buildings now restored or recreated, and the eighteenth-century atmosphere beautifully evoked with gardens, brick sidewalks, and old style signs and streetlighting, Salem is, as it originally was, a magnet for visitors and the epitome of Winston-Salem hospitality. Some 300,000 visit each year, including hundreds of groups of school children. It is, as it always was, a place where people live, work, and go to school. For the people of Winston-Salem, Old Salem is a vivid reminder of the values that built their city—industriousness, education, care for each person, and a love of order and beauty.

When plans for restoring Salem were starting to simmer, a bold and startling proposal for importing a cultural asset had already been launched. The story broke on March 25, 1946: the Z. Smith Reynolds Foundation had offered $350,000 a year in perpetuity to Wake Forest College, if it would move to Winston-Salem. The invitation included an offer of some 300 acres of land in the Reynolda area from Charles H. Babcock, a wealthy investment banker, and a $2 million challenge grant from William N. Neal and his niece Nancy Reynolds Babcock toward building expenses.

Though Wake Forest's medical school had earlier moved to Winston-Salem through a bequest from the estate of Bowman Gray, the idea of uprooting the entire college sent shock waves through the campus. Wake Forest was a well-regarded Baptist-supported institution, which had flourished in a small town in Wake County for more than 100 years.

But in the minds of William Reynolds (brother of the founder of R. J. Reynolds Tobacco Company) and the members of his family, Winston-Salem needed a Wake Forest. The city had a women's college, Salem, and a college for black students, Winston-Salem Teachers College (now Winston-Salem State University), but no college for white men. Reynolds, as a trustee of Duke University, had seen firsthand what a tobacco fortune could do for higher learning, and he seems to have felt that the Baptist support for Wake Forest would help in the enormous and expensive relocation project.

The college trustees eventually accepted the offer. By the time of the official groundbreaking ceremony, on a beautiful fall day in 1951, Will Reynolds had died, leaving another generous bequest to the college. President Harry S. Truman turned the first shovelful of earth on the new campus, and used the occasion to make a major foreign policy address.

Meeting the $3 million goal of the building fund, which was needed to claim the $2 million challenge grant, was a real challenge, and the people of Winston-Salem played their part. During the last six months of the drive, Twin Citians chipped in $846,000. The Reynolds Foundation also agreed to up its annual contribution to $500,000.

Moving Wake Forest took a decade. The new campus was built in a cost-conscious, modified Georgian style, but, even so, construction costs tripled original projections. When the first group of students were walking across newly planted grass to their brand new classrooms in the fall of 1956, Winston-Salem literally rolled out a red carpet at a gala "Salute to Wake Forest" at the new Memorial Coliseum. Ninety-eight local organizations sponsored the event, at which the histories of the college and the city were dramatized by a cast of hundreds, and the Winston-Salem Symphony, a Moravian band, and 200-voice choir performed for an audience of 6,000 people.

Will Reynolds' vision proved to be good for the growth of the college and the city. Wake Forest University enrolls more than 5,500 students in its college, graduate programs, and schools of business, law, and medicine. The university is one of the city's largest employers. The campus, now mellowed and mature looking, is still being built, the newer buildings adding welcome variety to the original architectural style. From the beginning, Wake Forest brought in a

welcome infusion of new people and intellectual stimulation and gave Winston-Salem something to cheer about—Wake's Demon Deacons have an avid following.

Winston-Salem's reputation as a thriving arts center is also the product of post-war endeavor. Before the war, the city depended heavily on visiting singers, musical ensembles, and opera companies for high quality entertainment. Between 1943 and 1950, the one fixed attraction in the cultural calendar was the Piedmont Festival, a week-long festival of opera, drama and musical performances, and exhibits of arts and crafts.

In 1945 the Junior League commissioned a survey of arts activities in the city, and in the following year both the Winston-Salem Civic Orchestra and the Winston-Salem Operetta Association were formed. As part of the county centennial, the cultural leaders of the city established the Winston-Salem Arts Council, generally acknowledged to be the first permanent arts council in the United States.

Over the years, the Arts Council has been effective in promoting and coordinating arts activities, and beginning in the late 1950s, in raising broadbased community financial support for its member organizations. Bringing the arts organizations under one umbrella set the stage for a full flowering and a national reputation in the 1970s and '80s.

While Piedmont Airlines was starting its passenger service and R. J. Reynolds Tobacco Company was on its way to dominating the new filter cigarette market with the development of its hometown namesake brands, Winston and Salem, the city was beginning to reap the fruits of its industry-hunting efforts. On an April day in 1946, some 2,500 people lined up in front of the old Chatham Manufacturing Company building to apply for jobs at Western

THE NEEDS OF BLACK CITIZENS BEGAN TO BE PART OF THE PUBLIC AGENDA. OBSTACLES TO VOTING WERE REMOVED, AND THE FIRST BLACK ALDERMAN SINCE RECONSTRUCTION DAYS, KENNETH R. WILLIAMS, WAS ELECTED. IN 1947 WINSTON-SALEM GOVERNMENT WAS LED BY (LEFT TO RIGHT) W. F. SHAFFNER JR., FRED C. DENNY, H. PENN THOMAS, C. F. BAUSERMAN, MAYOR GEORGE D. LENTZ, BAHNSON GRAY, FRANCIS D. PEPPER, KENNETH R. WILLIAMS, AND N. MOIR LANCASTER. PHOTO COURTESY OF PHOTO COLLECTION, FORSYTH COUNTY PUBLIC LIBRARY.

OPENED IN 1955, THRUWAY SHOPPING CENTER EMPHA-SIZED THE INFORMALITY AND CONVENIENCE OF A NEW WAY OF SHOPPING. PHOTO COURTESY OF PHOTO COLLECTION, FORSYTH COUNTY PUBLIC LIBRARY.

Electric. The company had been recruited to Winston-Salem by the director of the Chamber of Commerce, and by October, 1,600 people were employed at Western Electric, 90 percent of them hired locally. In 25 years Western Electric grew to be the county's second largest employer, with 7,000 on its payroll. It paved the way for other industries that required skilled labor, made union membership a fact of life in Winston-Salem, hired people from all over the country to work here, and gave the city a layer of technicians, engineers, and managers such as it had never had. With the coming of Western Electric, Winston-Salem could no longer be described as a city without a middle class, or a city of homegrown companies. The infusion of new blood showed up in the 1960 census—by then, 20 percent of people who lived in Winston-Salem had come from other places.

Unionization efforts forced Winston-Salem's white leadership to look at race problems for the first time. In the early 1940s, the Food, Tobacco, and Agricultural Workers Union sent organizers to Winston-Salem. Working through the black churches, they succeeded in establishing a union at Reynolds Tobacco. The local was short-lived—its leaders were identified as card-carrying Communists, which disqualified them from representing the employees—but another unionization attempt was made at Reynolds in 1947.

The union threat made the dissatis-faction of blacks highly visible. Two well respected community leaders, James G. Hanes and Joe Rice, asked

the Rockefeller Foundation in 1948 to finance a study of race relations in Winston-Salem. When the study was completed, a biracial committee began working to alleviate the problems that had been identified.

The needs of black citizens began to be part of the public agenda. Obstacles to voting were removed, and the first black alderman since Reconstruction days, Kenneth R. Williams, was elected. When the 1950 census showed that 39 percent of dwelling units in the city were either "deteriorating" or "dilapidated," the city formulated a comprehensive development plan, which included clearing blighted inner-city neighborhoods as well as rehabilitating the downtown and building new roads.

Urban renewal was a mixed blessing for the black community. Whole neigh-borhoods were razed, obliterating terrible slums and significant landmarks alike. The major roads built in the post-war period also had the effect of erasing black history, as they cut through the older and more prosperous black neigh-borhoods. Black churches, business buildings, and historic homes fell to the bulldozers. In time, much of the cleared land was rebuilt, with housing units much safer and more comfortable than the majority of those they replaced, and with public service buildings and com-munity centers. But urban renewal took a toll on Winston-Salem's black community, at a time when blacks had no political power to prevent the devas-tation of their traditions and history.

Physical improvements were made to the all-black schools. Full desegregation was years off, but in 1957, when 15-year-old Gwendolyn Bailey was assigned to be the first black student at Reynolds High School, James G. Hanes made sure that this token integration would be a peaceful one.

Hanes called 40 city leaders to a meeting at his house and urged their cooperation. "This is no longer a matter of our likes and dislikes," he told them.

"It is a matter of law and what we must do. What I am asking of you is your help in seeing that it is done, and done quietly."

As it had in earlier years, philanthropy benefited black citizens as well as white. Winston Lake Park, a recreation area for blacks, was developed with gifts from the Z. Smith Reynolds Foundation, Wachovia, Hanes, and Reynolds Tobacco. The Dixie Classic Fairgrounds came into being with a grant from the Winston-Salem Foundation, and the city's minor league baseball field, Ernie Shore Field, was a donation from Charles Babcock. Charles and Mary Reynolds Babcock also donated land on Reynolda Road for Summit School, which by 1946 had outgrown its original home in the West End.

Winston-Salem still faced downtown in the post-war years. Townspeople and farmers flocked to the City Market on Saturdays. Department stores, movie theaters, and restaurants drew people to the center for shopping and entertainment. The Hotel Robert E. Lee was the place to go for family Sunday dinners, for dances on the rooftop, to see the display of live chicks at Easter, and for regular meetings of more than a dozen civic clubs. Sosnik's department store, in an old building handsomely renovated by Raymond Loewy, drew shoppers from as far away as Atlanta for its elegant merchandise and its unparalleled ambience. The K & W, Winston-Salem's perennially popular cafeteria, was downtown then, drugstores had soda fountains, and tea rooms provided refreshment for shoppers and office workers. The Reynolds headquarters building dominated the skyline, and the sweet smell of tobacco from its downtown factories permeated the air. Even the city's new television station had a home in the center; WSJS (later renamed WXII-TV) began broadcasting from the *Journal and Sentinel* building in time for the 1951 World Series.

Nevertheless, it was to the suburbs that people were moving, and the suburban lifestyle brought changes of its own. An exciting development was Thruway, the first shopping center outside of downtown, which opened in 1955. Thruway emphasized the informality and convenience of this new way of shopping, and was an immediate success. After Thruway, 14 more shopping centers opened in the next 10 years.

A suburban location was chosen for the James G. Hanes Community Center, which opened in 1958. The $1 million center was built to house three of the city's most important organizations: the Chamber of Commerce; the United Fund; and the Arts Council, which then had 22 members. (Interestingly, all three have since moved their headquarters back downtown). Business, charity, and culture—these were Winston-Salem's pride, and the drive to raise the money to build Hanes Community Center was one of 16 capital campaigns mounted in the 10 years after the war.

The campaigns all followed a winning formula: outstanding leadership, usually provided by the top executives of the big companies, and second and third generations of their founding families; lead gifts provided by local philanthropic foundations and large corporations; and smaller contributions from thousands of individuals. Pre-war paternalism had been replaced with broadbased community support, but the vision and the leadership still came from a small, tightly knit group.

"Clearing it with the 19th floor of the Reynolds building" was the shorthand expression for how decisions were made in Winston-Salem. The men who ran the big companies had a powerful say in what would be built in Winston-Salem and where the roads would run. They were the community leaders, and they were the government leaders, too, a dominant presence on the Board of Aldermen, the Board of Commissioners, and in the state legislature.

Winston-Salem was selected as an All-America City in 1959. Like many cities, it had undertaken massive improvement and public building projects that were much needed after the relatively fallow period of depression and war. Like other communities, it had turned to professional management of local government and professional planning of growth and development. But Winston-Salem carved out a special place for itself by building on its unique roots. In the preservation of Old Salem, in the relocation of Wake Forest, in the coordinating of its arts organizations, the City of Industry had blossomed into a city of culture. In presenting the Twin City's case to the All-America City Award Jury, Dr. Dale Gramley, then president of Salem College, stressed Winston-Salem's cooperative efforts in "restoring its past, improving its present, and blueprinting its future." ❖

IN 1957 GWENDOLYN BAILEY WAS ASSIGNED TO BE THE FIRST BLACK STUDENT AT REYNOLDS HIGH SCHOOL. PHOTO COURTESY OF PHOTO COLLECTION, FORSYTH COUNTY PUBLIC LIBRARY.

Chapter 6

✣

An All-America City

(1961-1983)

THE ALL-AMERICA CITY
DESIGNATION WAS A FITTING
BIRTHDAY TRIBUTE WHEN
WINSTON-SALEM CELEBRATED
ITS BICENTENNIAL IN 1966.

✤

PHOTO COURTESY OF PHOTO
COLLECTION, FORSYTH COUNTY
PUBLIC LIBRARY.

*T*wo momentous events in education tested Winston-Salem's cooperative spirit in the 1960s and '70s. The first was the competition for a new conservatory for professional training in the performing arts. The conservatory was the dream of Governor Terry Sanford, who was elected in 1960, and his brilliant cultural aide, the novelist John Ehle. They understood that nurturing the talent of young artists could not be accomplished within the traditional high school and university structure, and they set about creating the first state-supported residential school for the performing arts in the United States.

The idea of the "tippy toe school," as some state legislators characterized it, was not easy to grasp, as there were no models of it in America. But as the plan was fleshed out, and legislated into existence by the N.C. General Assembly, the major cities in North Carolina began to see the advantages of having the

innovative institution within their boundaries, and they were all invited to submit proposals for offering facilities and raising the money to start a campus.

Compared to Raleigh, the state capital, and Charlotte, the largest city in the Carolinas, Winston-Salem seemed a dark horse at best. R. Philip Hanes Jr., an early advocate of getting the school for Winston-Salem, looked at the possibilities of acquiring Graylyn, Reynolda House, or the old City Hospital for the conservatory site. But when it came time to actually make a proposal, all Winston-Salem had to offer was the old Gray High School building on the south side of town. It would take $900,000 to make the building usable for an arts school.

Two weeks before a site selection committee was due to gather in North Carolina and visit all the interested cities, Smith Bagley and Philip Hanes came up with the idea of raising almost $1 million over the phone. Having the needed funds already in hand when the

FOR ALMOST 30 YEARS, THE NORTH CAROLINA SCHOOL OF THE ARTS HAS TRAINED DANCERS, MUSICIANS, ACTORS, DIRECTORS, PLAYWRIGHTS, VISUAL ARTISTS, STAGE MANAGERS, AND LIGHTING, COSTUME, AND SCENE DESIGNERS. PICTURED HERE, THE SCHOOL PERFORMS **THE NUTCRACKER**. PHOTO COURTESY OF PHOTO COLLECTION, FORSYTH COUNTY PUBLIC LIBRARY.

THE GOVERNOR'S SCHOOL, A SUMMER
PROGRAM FOR OUTSTANDING HIGH
SCHOOL JUNIORS AND SENIORS FROM
ACROSS THE STATE OF NORTH
CAROLINA, BEGAN IN 1963 ON THE
CAMPUS OF SALEM COLLEGE. PHOTO
COURTESY OF PHOTO COLLECTION,
FORSYTH COUNTY PUBLIC LIBRARY.

committee made its decision seemed a
sure way of making the case for
Winston-Salem. Knowing that such an
ambitious, zero-hour campaign would
require total community backing, they
enlisted the newspaper, radio, and television support to drum up interest in
the city. Four days before the committee
was due to visit, they kicked off the
fund-raising campaign at a Chamber
of Commerce Coffee Club, passing
out checks on local banks, which most
of the 200 people present signed on
the condition that the checks would
be returned if the $900,000 goal
wasn't achieved.

The two-day Dial for Dollars campaign began on the morning of April 28,
1963. More than 200 volunteers had
been enlisted to man phone banks at
Hanes Community Center. The selection
committee arrived at the community
center late that morning, toured the city
and the Gray High School site, and left
that afternoon to see what Greensboro
had to offer, with copies of the morning's *Journal*, which carried the front
page headline "Give Us the School."

Choreographer Agnes de Mille,
one of the committee members, was
impressed with the fervent and

intelligent support she saw in
Winston-Salem. "It's new here (in
America)," she commented later, "this
kind of communal enthusiasm for something that is so important and so
absolutely unprofitable, except in the
spiritual sense."

The next night, even before the
successful phone campaign (to which
over 5,000 people contributed) was
over, the committee chose Winston-
Salem. The actor Sidney Blackmer, who
was chairman, explained, ". . . we were
chiefly influenced, I think, by the spirit
of the citizens. Everyone seemed to
respond . . . 'This is what we want!'"

The North Carolina School of the Arts
got its name that same night, and it
opened in the fall of 1965, with compos-
er Vittorio Giannini as its first president.
For almost 30 years, the school has
trained dancers, musicians, actors, directors, playwrights, visual artists, stage
managers, and lighting, costume, and
scene designers. A School of
Filmmaking has recently been added to
the Schools of Music, Dance, Drama,
and Design and Production. The school's
successful alumni include Peter Hedges,
author of *What's Eating Gilbert Grape?*,
Tom Hulce, star of the movie *Amadeus*,
Terrence Mann, star of the Broadway
hits *Cats* and *Beauty and the Beast*, Mel
Tomlinson, soloist with the New York
City Ballet, choreographer Peter Pucci,
flutist Ransom Wilson, cellist Sharon
Robinson, and opera singers John Cheek
and Gianna Rolandi, among many,
many more.

The School of the Arts secured
Winston-Salem's claim to cultural emi-
nence. Guided by a faculty of about 100
distinguished artist-teachers, and
enriched by residencies of another 100
visiting artists each year, the school
annually presents some 300 public performances of music, dance, and drama in
Winston-Salem. In addition to its own
presentations, the school enhances the
quality of every arts organization in the
city. The Winston-Salem Piedmont Triad
Symphony, Piedmont Opera Theatre,

IN 1966, AS A PART OF THE CITY'S BICENTENNIAL CERE-
MONIES, STATE AND LOCAL OFFICIALS WERE ON HAND TO
COMMEMORATE THE FIRST OFFICIAL FOURTH OF JULY
CELEBRATION HELD IN SALEM. PHOTO COURTESY OF
PHOTO COLLECTION, FORSYTH COUNTY PUBLIC LIBRARY.

North Carolina Black Repertory Company, the Little Theatre, Piedmont Chamber Singers, and smaller performing arts organizations all benefit from the talents of people who teach or have been taught at the North Carolina School of the Arts. Many of Winston-Salem's arts groups came into existence as the direct result of the school's location here.

While Winston-Salem was vying for the arts school, two other innovative educational ventures were given a home in Winston-Salem—the Governor's School and the Advancement School. Both were also conceived by Terry Sanford and John Ehle. The Governor's School, a summer program for outstanding high school juniors and seniors from across the state, began in 1963 on the campus of Salem College. The $225,000 needed to match the Carnegie Corporation grant for this project was raised in 10 minutes, at a meeting of the usual group of community leaders and benefactors. From the beginning it has been a national model for programs in education of gifted students and has been so successful that it was expanded to a second campus to serve more students, at Saint Andrew's Presbyterian College in Laurinburg. The North Carolina Advancement School, a residential school for underachieving eighth graders, was opened in 1965 in the former City Hospital building and pioneered strategies for serving this kind of student for the several years it operated.

Education was the highlight of Winston-Salem's second successful application to be an All-America City in 1964. Besides having won for itself the three special state schools, the city had a new technical school, Winston-Salem/Forsyth County Industrial Education Center (later Forsyth Technical Institute and now Forsyth Technical Community College), a new Nature-Science Center (now SciWorks), and had raised money to build Salem College Fine Arts Center, to expand the

Bowman Gray School of Medicine, and to build a dormitory for Goodwill Industries' trainees. The dollar value of the city's educational improvements totaled over $10 million.

The All-America City designation was, as it was intended to be, a fitting birthday tribute when Winston-Salem celebrated its bicentennial in 1966. The year-long celebration began in January with a Festival of Thanksgiving at Memorial Auditorium and ended in December with the first presentation of *The Nutcracker* ballet by students of the new School of the Arts.

The people of Winston-Salem had rallied in support of educational ventures they saw as desirable for the city's reputation and its future. A much harder test of the cooperative spirit came in 1971, when the community was ordered by a federal court to immediately and totally desegregate its public schools.

School desegregation had begun in the late '50s and was furthered after the passage of the Civil Rights Act of 1964, by which time the city and county schools were consolidated. After the filing of a suit on behalf of Catherine Scott and other students in the late '60s, the school board proposed a variety of pupil assignment plans to try to satisfy the demands of the courts without creating total havoc in the educational system. In 1970 a federal judge's decision against the latest plan was appealed to the United States Supreme Court, where the decision was upheld.

Ultimately, in June of 1971, the school board was given 10 days to produce a pupil assignment plan that would effect full desegregation. During that period, teams of school administrators were literally locked in rooms as they tried to design a plan that would make all 64 schools in the system racially balanced in about the same proportions as the system as a whole, 70 percent white and 30 percent black. Given the city's and county's very segregated housing patterns, and the locations of the schools, it proved impossible to come up with a workable plan for either three-year or four-year high schools. The plan that the courts approved and ordered into effect on July 26, one month before school was scheduled to open, gave Winston-Salem and Forsyth County a public education structure undoubtedly unique in the nation. In the course of 12 grades, all students would attend five different schools, four of them for two years each.

The best anyone could say of the court-approved plan was that it was equally unfair to everybody. It eliminated neighborhood schools, introduced massive and expensive cross-busing, destroyed continuity in sports, arts, and all extracurricular activities, disrupted the lives of all families with children in public schools, and from an educational point of view, made no sense at all.

But once it was clear to the community that the courts absolutely required the abrupt and massive change, most people turned their attention to making the plan work. Citizens councils, civic organizations, churches, parents, and teachers worked together to make the transition as peaceful and positive as possible. During the first difficult year, parents rode the school buses, volunteered in distant and unfamiliar schools, patrolled the hallways and cafeterias, and formed organizations to hear and deal with complaints and problems, which were relatively few and minor. School superintendent Marvin Ward (who after his retirement in 1976 went on to serve as a state senator) emerged

as a strong and effective leader, guiding the community through the first five years of full integration.

Ten years after the August day when almost 32,500 pupils were first bused out of their neighborhoods, more integrated housing patterns were allowing consideration of a plan to finally establish four-year high schools and six-year elementary schools. Black and white parents and teachers alike agreed that much had been sacrificed to achieve school integration. The universally loathed 4-2-2-2-2 grade structure had proved to be as educationally unsound as everyone had feared it would be, but the people of Winston-Salem had exhibited a considerable amount of grace under very unwelcome pressure.

In 1981 Marvin Calloway, who was the school board chairman then and who had been a PTA leader 10 years earlier, summed it up: "We did something nobody wanted to do, and we did it peacefully."

While the schools were radically restructuring, the downtown area was also feeling the effects of change. The Wachovia Bank Building, a modern 30-story skyscraper which opened in 1966, now dominated the skyline, and the newly constructed stretch of Interstate 40, by city officials' choice, ran right beside the central business district. But the older, communal identity of the center of the city was gradually disappearing. The City Market closed, and on a March day in 1972, thousands of people gathered to witness the demise

THE BUILDINGS THAT WERE ERECTED DOWNTOWN IN THE LATE '60S AND THE '70S WERE OFFICE BUILDINGS AND PUBLIC BUILDINGS. DOWNTOWN CAME TO BE ENVISIONED AS WHAT IT IS TODAY, A BUSINESS, GOVERNMENT, AND CONVENTION DISTRICT ENLIVENED BY A CLUSTER OF ARTS ACTIVITIES. A PANORAMIC VIEW OF MARSHALL AND FIFTH STREETS IN 1971 SHOWS (LEFT TO RIGHT) BENTON CONVENTION CENTER, REYNOLDS BUILDING, HOTEL ROBERT E. LEE, NISSEN BUILDING, AND SECURITY LIFE (NOW INTEGON). PHOTO COURTESY OF PHOTO COLLECTION, FORSYTH COUNTY PUBLIC LIBRARY.

of one of their most cherished land-marks. The Hotel Robert E. Lee was reduced to rubble in less than 10 seconds when 300 sticks of dynamite were set off in its basement. A chain hotel replaced the Robert E. Lee, and a chain department store replaced Sosnik's, the unique, locally owned department store on Fourth Street.

The opening of Hanes Mall, which was built on farmland out Stratford Road, was the beginning of the end of downtown as a retail center. Controversial in the planning stages, the mall quickly became almost a way of life for thousands of people, not only from Winston-Salem but from much of the northwest region of the state also. A big center when it opened, it was expanded in the late 1980s, making it the largest mall in the Carolinas.

The buildings that were erected downtown in the late '60s and the '70s were office buildings and public buildings, including two hotels, the Benton Convention Center, the Wachovia and North Carolina National Bank (now NationsBank) buildings, Integon Insurance, the County Hall of Justice, and the Federal Building. The *Winston-Salem Journal and Sentinel* remained downtown, though they were no longer locally owned, but the company's "children," WSJS Radio and WXII Television, moved away from the center. Between the office buildings and the old churches, many small restaurants and shops came and went. Although there was discussion and experimentation in regard to reviving downtown as a shopping and living area, these efforts were largely unsuccessful. Downtown came to be envisioned as what it is today, a business, government, and convention district enlivened by a cluster of arts activities.

The old neighborhoods surrounding downtown had a shabby and neglected look by the mid '60s, with many of the grand old houses divided up and converted to rental properties and boarding houses. The neighborhood

association movement, which swept the country in the early 1970s, can be credited with preserving Winston-Salem's old housing stock and revitalizing the center city neighborhoods. Neighborhood associations sprung up, first in the West End, later in the downtown area now called Crystal Towers, and in Washington Park, Ardmore, and the West Salem and Crafton Heights areas. At first unaided by any public support, small groups of people in each neighborhood organized their neighbors, fought for zoning changes, resisted attempts to raze old buildings and to replace residential buildings with commercial enterprises, bought threatened houses, worked with absentee landlords, found people to buy and live in dilapidated houses, and on weekends and evenings, helped each other plaster, paint, plumb, and landscape. By banding together and taking on city hall, the neighborhood organizers were able to enlist public support, including federal community development money to provide low interest loans to rehabilitate the city's oldest existing neighborhoods. By the late 1970s, Washington Park and the large West End neighborhood were again fashionable addresses. No longer shunned by real estate agents and mortgage companies, the old neighborhoods, with their interesting residential architecture, tree-shaded streets, and pretty parks, became sources of civic pride and interest. The neighborhood associations, with all their internal disagreements and powerful foes, have been strong models of cooperation, between young and old, lifelong residents and city newcomers, government and private interests.

The neighborhood movement was but one indication that power was moving into the hands of a much broader base of people. All the local governmental boards, for so long dominated by members of old families and executives of the major corporations, were now peopled with newcomers, women, and blacks. The city watched, with some dismay, as the old closed-door

THE O'KELLY LIBRARY AT WINSTON-SALEM STATE UNIVERSITY IS HOME TO THE DIGGS GALLERY, WHICH FOCUSES ON THE WORK OF AFRICAN-AMERICAN ARTISTS. PHOTO COURTESY OF PHOTO COLLECTION, FORSYTH COUNTY PUBLIC LIBRARY.

consensus and "clearing it with the 19th floor of the Reynolds building" way of doing public business gave way to a more open, combative, and often agonizingly prolonged style of making decisions. Spreading leadership around has been a lengthy and often frustrating process in Winston-Salem.

Many of the changes the '70s brought took the city in the direction of Anytown, USA—the chain stores at the mall, the fast food outlets along Stratford Road, Peter's Creek Parkway, and other strips, the bland-looking schools and hospitals and other public buildings, the cookie-cutter housing developments, and the new "liquor by the drink" law that took people out of their homes and private clubs for more public socializing at a growing array of bars and restaurants. What set Winston-Salem apart, as the decade drew to a close, was an astonishing wealth of high culture.

In the 1970s, Winston-Salem came to the realization that its bountiful supply of arts events could be the means of building a community, revitalizing its downtown, attracting tourists, and luring new industry. Downtown street festivals, most prominently Carolina StreetScene and MayFest, sponsored by the Arts Council, were hugely popular annual events during the 1970s and '80s. The North Carolina Dance Theatre, Piedmont Opera Theatre, and the North Carolina Shakespeare Festival in nearby High Point all started as affiliates of the North Carolina School of the Arts and provided regular performances of excellent quality. The Winston-Salem Symphony, which had been an orchestra of gifted amateurs, rose to new artistic levels with the direction of Peter Perret and the infusion of teachers and graduates of the School of the Arts, and expanded its traditional offerings with children's concerts and a pops series. In 1979 Larry Leon Hamlin founded the North Carolina Black Repertory Company, giving Winston-Salem yet another fully professional performing arts organization.

Museums and galleries thrived. The Southeastern Center for Contemporary Art (SECCA) became a national as well as a local force when it moved in 1972 to the English country-style home of the late James G. Hanes, to which a striking contemporary gallery space was added. Reynolda House became a museum of American art in 1965, and the Sawtooth Center, in an old textile mill, was made into a home for visual arts organizations, studios, and galleries. In Old Salem a nondescript supermarket had been transformed into the Museum of Early Southern Decorative Arts, a series of rooms reconstructed from Southern houses in the 1690-1820 period, each authentically exhibiting the furniture, textiles, pottery, and art of its particular time and place. Since it opened in 1965, MESDA has been a nationally acclaimed center of research into antique furnishings. African and African-American art and educational programs were displayed and offered at the Delta Fine Arts Center. The annual fair presented by Piedmont Craftsmen, a highly respected regional guild of master potters, woodworkers, and metal and fiber artists, grew to be an enormous three-day event.

Capping Winston-Salem's emergence as the "Athens of the South" was the opening of the Roger L. Stevens Center for the Performing Arts. The Carolina Theatre and Hotel building had been given to the School of the Arts by Piedmont Publishing Company (which had its *Journal and Sentinel* newspaper operations in the same block), and the old movie palace had undergone a $10 million renovation, with federal money and many private donations. Gregory Peck was the master of ceremonies at the gala opening in April 1983. Leonard Bernstein conducted the student orchestra and Isaac Stern was the violin soloist. Along with the long list of luminaries on stage that night, the capacity audience included former President and Mrs. Gerald Ford, former First Lady Lady Bird Johnson,

and scores of representatives of the national art world and media.

In the years just ahead, Winston-Salem would find itself in the national spotlight on many more occasions, not all of them so triumphant. ✛

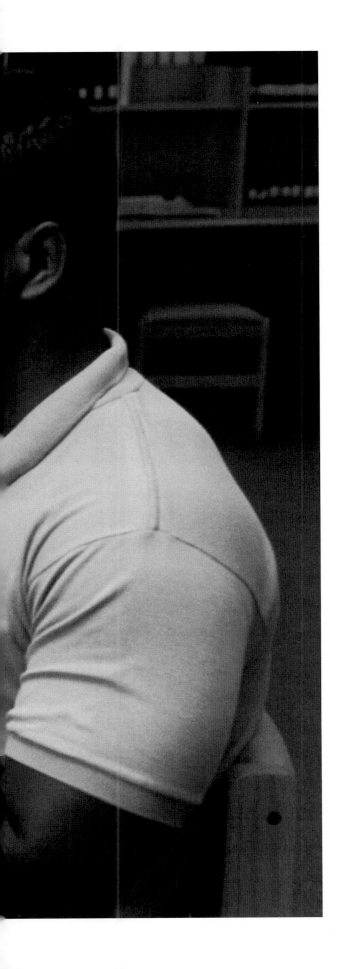

Chapter 7

✛

Toward a Common Vision
(1984-1994)

RACIAL HARMONY WAS A PRIORITY FOR
THE COMMUNITY IN THE LAST DECADE
OF THE CENTURY, AND EVERYWHERE
PEOPLE WERE TRYING TO PUT THE
LONG TRADITION OF EXCLUSION AND
SEGREGATION IN THE PAST.

✛

PHOTO COURTESY OF WINSTON-SALEM
STATE UNIVERSITY.

On the evening of Friday, May 5, 1989, without warning, a series of tornadoes struck Winston-Salem, throwing much of the city into darkness and confusion. People woke the next morning to a clear, bright day and the sound of chain saws. During the weekend, thousands made their way through streets clogged with fallen trees and utility poles, trying to find open restaurants and grocery stores, or checking on families and friends in the worst affected neighborhoods. The devastation that met their eyes was shocking—familiar streets had become unrecognizable, and even the venerable trees on Salem Square were torn out by their roots.

It looked worse than it was, though damages totaled $50 million. For all its brief ferocity, the storm had claimed no lives. Within days, electrical power, water, and phone service were restored to most parts of the city. New trees were planted, and in a matter of months most of the afflicted houses were looking better than they had before the storm.

The damage was so quickly repaired that the tornado of 1989 is no more than a footnote in the history of Winston-Salem. But the feelings of shock, disorientation, and grief the tornado briefly stirred were familiar to Winston-Salem by 1989. In that decade of mergers and acquistions and corporate upheavals,

Winston-Salem had felt storms shaking every one of its major companies. The Hanes companies were now part of Sara Lee Corporation. Piedmont Airlines had merged into USAIR and lost its primary connection to its hometown. The locally-based trucking companies, Pilot Freight, Hennis, and McLean, had not survived. AT&T had announced the closing of one its large plants in the city, a loss of some 3,000 jobs. Wachovia's merger with First Atlanta triggered rumors that the bank might desert its hometown headquarters. The waves of corporate "downsizings" that would continue for years were beginning.

The worst blow came in the early days of 1987. Ever since the end of 1985, when R. J. Reynolds Industries acquired Nabisco Foods, people in Winston-Salem had been wondering "who bought whom?" When one of the Nabisco people, Ross Johnson, became CEO on January 1, 1987, the question seemed to be answered. Two weeks later, the rumors that had been buzzing for a year were confirmed: RJR Nabisco was leaving town, moving its headquarters to Atlanta.

The RJR Nabisco headquarters move did more damage to the city's ego than its economy. About 300 jobs moved, but the tobacco company, which had 14,000 on its payroll, remained. The company donated its glass headquarters building at Whitaker Park to Wake Forest University, and announced plans to move its Planters LifeSavers division to Winston-Salem. Local citizens reacted strongly against a national newspaper's characterization of Winston-Salem as a "company town" and to Ross Johnson's description of the Twin City as a "bucolic" spot. Business

ON THE EVENING OF FRIDAY, MAY 5, 1989, A SERIES OF TORNADOES STRUCK WINSTON-SALEM. THE DEVASTATION WAS SHOCKING—FAMILIAR STREETS HAD BECOME UNRECOGNIZABLE, AND EVEN THE VENERABLE TREES IN OLD SALEM WERE TORN APART. PHOTO BY ALISON HUFF.

leaders worked hard to present a brighter and truer image of Winston-Salem to the 60 news crews that descended on the city.

It looked worse than it was, but the RJR move precipitated serious scrutiny of what Winston-Salem had become and where it was headed. Around tables in the new Piedmont Club on the top floor of Winston's latest skyscraper, One Triad Park, and in boardrooms, living rooms, and the pages of the media, self-examination was the order of the day. A bucolic company town whose glory days were over? A future as a neighborhood in a sprawling metropolitan area called the Piedmont Triad? An eventual suburb of Kernersville? Or something yet to be imagined?

IN A DECADE OF MERGERS AND ACQUISITIONS AND CORPORATE UPHEAVALS, WINSTON-SALEM HAD FELT STORMS SHAKING EVERY ONE OF ITS MAJOR COMPANIES INCLUDING R. J. REYNOLDS. SHOWN HERE IS THE WHITAKER PARK MANUFACTURING CENTER IN 1992. PHOTO COURTESY OF R. J. REYNOLDS TOBACCO COMPANY.

In the mid-1990s, Winston-Salem had answered some of those questions. The serious efforts begun in the late '80s to keep and expand the companies it had and to attract new industries were paying off. Winston-Salem was defining when "Triadism" made sense, and when it was better to stand on its own merits. The medical industry was proving to be one of Winston-Salem's healthiest. By the early '90s the Bowman Gray/Baptist Hospital Medical Center was the city's second largest employer, was becoming a center of research in new areas, including aging, human nutrition, and disease prevention, and was home to Brenner's Children's Hospital. Forsyth Memorial Hospital, now owned and managed by Carolina Medicorp, Inc., had grown to include a women's health care center and a state-of-the-art rehabilitation center. A new Wachovia headquarters building was under construction downtown. And people were speculating that Winston-Salem might be on its way to becoming the "Hollywood of the South," as the new Winston-Salem Piedmont Triad Film Commission began aggressively wooing moviemakers with the area's abundant variety of locations, the new film school at the School of the Arts geared up, and the Chamber of Commerce actively promoted the building of a multimedia studio.

By the mid-1990s, Winston-Salem's cooperative spirit had taken a more creative turn. As it emerged from the doldrums of the '80s, the city began giving birth to a series of ventures characterized by new collaborations, imaginative reworkings of old institutions, familiar places, and interesting partnerships. The old City Market was one example: the building was renovated to hold not only an outdoor food market again, but also offices for architects and other professionals, the Winston-Salem Visitor Center, and an innovative elementary school, founded with a grant from the RJR Nabisco Foundation and operated by the public school system. Around the market, an interesting arts

district came into being, where dozens of artists and craftsmen had their studios, galleries, and shops.

The southeastern quadrant of the city was in the first stages of a major facelift. Home to Old Salem, Salem College and Academy, Winston-Salem State University, and the North Carolina School of the Arts, this old part of the city was a jumble of confusing roads, vacant lots, and dilapidated buildings. Through the cooperation of the neighboring institutions and private citizens, the Southeast Gateway project was launched, a plan for bringing cohesion and focus to the area, and making it attractive to students, tourists, and residents of the Washington Park and Happy Hills neighborhoods.

Racial harmony was a priority for the community in the last decade of the century, and everywhere people were trying to put the long tradition of exclusion and segregation in the past. One of the ongoing events that brought out highly visible cooperation was the National Black Theatre Festival, which was founded by the North Carolina Black Repertory Company. Held in 1989, 1991, and 1993, the festival brought thousands of African-American performers to stages all over the city, and attracted the attention of every major news organization in the country. Chairmen of the festival in those years were Maya Angelou, Ruby Dee, Ossie Davis, Sidney Poitier, Della Reese, and Harry Belafonte. Hundreds of black and white volunteers worked to make the festival a success, and it received the financial support of the city's major corporations.

Twenty-five years ago the people who charted Winston-Salem's course

WINSTON-SALEM JOURNAL

At Least 3 Killed as Tornadoes Rip Across Carolina

Electricity Lines And Trees Down Across Piedmont

Storms Kill at Least 2 People in South Carolina

were a remarkably homogeneous group, and almost without exception, white, male, and wealthy. Perhaps nothing is more indicative of how much more inclusive and diverse the community has become than the list of the board of directors of Leadership Winston-Salem. Since 1984 this non-profit organization has educated leaders in every field of endeavor about the issues facing the community and the differing points of view on those issues. More than 300 people have participated in this illuminating training; there can be no doubt that they are bringing a truly community-wide perspective into all of the city's institutions.

Winston-Salem honors the ideal of working together for the common good in its hyphenated name and in its motto. In every stage of its development, the city founded upon cooperation has struggled to incorporate new groups of people and clashing points of view. Its history teaches that working together has always required effort, goodwill, and perseverance. Its present offers new opportunities for revealing a cooperative spirit. ✥

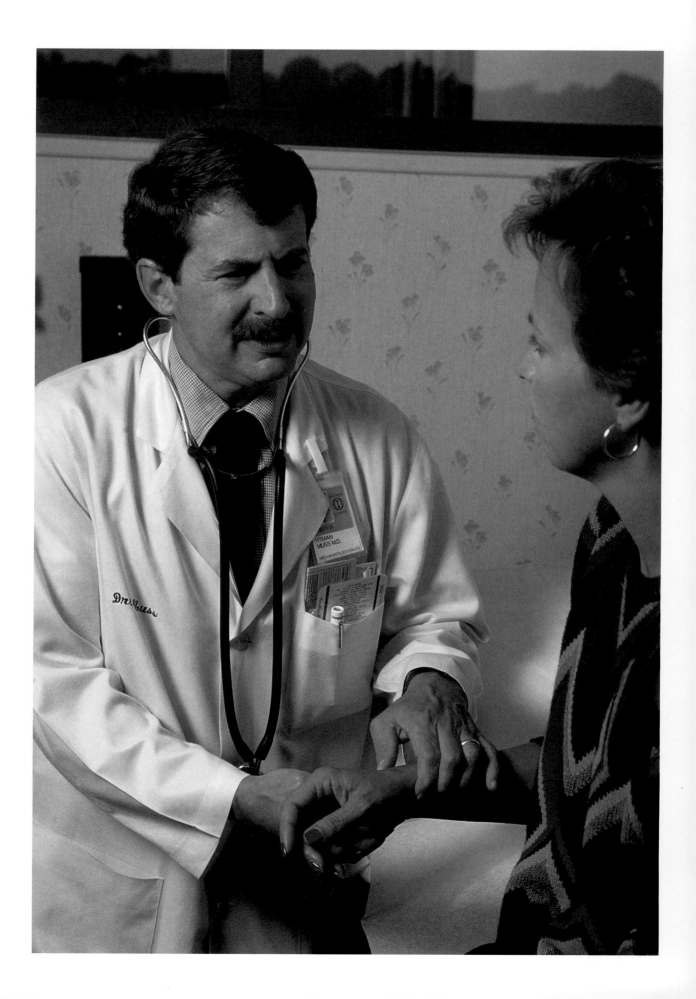

(PREVIOUS PAGE) DR. HYMAN B. MUSS OF THE BOWMAN GRAY SCHOOL OF MEDICINE OF WAKE FOREST UNIVERSITY WAS RECOGNIZED BY **GOOD HOUSEKEEPING** MAGAZINE IN 1992 AS ONE OF THE TOP DOCTORS FOR THE TREATMENT OF BREAST AND GYNECOLOGICAL CANCERS. PHOTO BY WILL & DENI MCINTYRE

THE SOUTHERN NATIONAL FINANCE CENTER (FORMERLY ONE TRIAD PARK) ADDS TO THE BEAUTY OF DOWNTOWN WINSTON-SALEM. PHOTO BY MIKE MAHER.

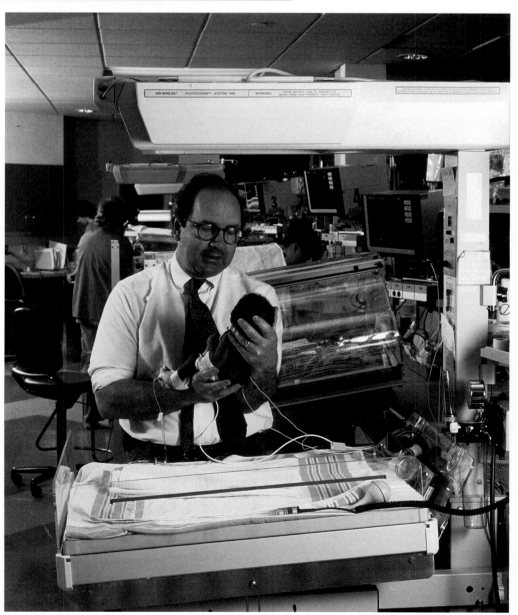

IN THE '90S, THE MEDICAL INDUSTRY WAS PROVING TO BE ONE OF WINSTON-SALEM'S HEALTHIEST EMPLOYERS. SHOWN HERE, A DOCTOR AT FORSYTH MEMORIAL HOSPITAL EXAMINES ONE OF THE COMMUNITY'S NEWEST CITIZENS. PHOTO COURTESY OF FORSYTH MEMORIAL HOSPITAL.

THE NORTH CAROLINA SCHOOL OF THE ARTS IS ONE OF THE FINEST EXAMPLES OF WINSTON-SALEM'S COOPERATIVE SPIRIT. PHOTO BY C. BUCHANAN.

THE NATIONAL BLACK THEATRE FESTIVAL, WHICH WAS FOUNDED BY THE NORTH CAROLINA BLACK REPERTORY COMPANY, BRINGS THOUSANDS OF AFRICAN-AMERICAN PERFORMERS TO STAGES ALL OVER THE CITY. HUNDREDS OF BLACK AND WHITE VOLUNTEERS WORK TO MAKE THE FESTIVAL A SUCCESS. PICTURED IS **CELEBRATIONS: AN AFRICAN ODYSSEY.** PHOTO BY RICARDO PITTS-WILEY.

Maestro Peter Perret conducts the Winston-Salem Piedmont Triad Symphony. Photo courtesy of the Winston-Salem Piedmont Triad Symphony.

Kathryn Crosby, along with the members of the tournament's board of directors, is shown at the closing ceremonies of the 1993 Crosby National Celebrity/ Charity Golf Tournament. Photo by Bernard Carpenter.

THE SOUTHEASTERN CENTER FOR CONTEMPORARY ART (SECCA) IS HOUSED IN THE
ENGLISH COUNTRY-STYLE HOME OF THE LATE JAMES G. HANES. A STRIKING CONTEMPO-
RARY GALLERY SPACE HAS BEEN ADDED. PHOTO COURTESY OF SECCA.

GRAYLYN, A STONE NORMAN REVIVAL STRUCTURE
AND FORMER HOME OF BOWMAN GRAY, IS TODAY
OWNED BY WAKE FOREST UNIVERSITY AND IS AN
AWARD-WINNING, INTERNATIONAL CONFERENCE
CENTER. PHOTO COURTESY OF GRAYLYN
INTERNATIONAL CONFERENCE CENTER OF WAKE
FOREST UNIVERSITY.

REYNOLDA HOUSE, THE FORMER COUNTRY ESTATE OF R. J. AND KATHARINE REYNOLDS, BECAME A
MUSEUM OF AMERICAN ART IN 1965. PHOTO COURTESY OF REYNOLDA HOUSE MUSEUM OF
AMERICAN ART.

MUSIC REMAINS A CORNERSTONE OF LIFE IN OLD SALEM TODAY.

HOME MORAVIAN CHURCH WAS DEDICATED NOVEMBER 9, 1800. THE CHURCH HAS OPERATED CONTINUOUSLY SINCE THAT TIME AND TODAY HAS MORE THAN 1,000 ACTIVE MEMBERS FROM THE WINSTON-SALEM COMMUNITY. PHOTO BY ALISON HUFF.

Partners in Progess

Winston-Salem's development is made vivid and dynamic in the stories of its businesses and institutions. When and why they were established and how they changed and grew gives us a picture of the community's values and tastes and opportunities and needs in every period of its history.

Some of Winston's wagonmakers became manufacturers of furniture when automobiles put horses and buggies out of business.

Much of Winston-Salem's wealth was created when the manufacturers of chewing tobacco accurately foresaw a huge market for smoking tobacco. The development of the city's educational institutions mirrors changing attitudes about who should be educated and what they need to learn.

In a city that prides itself on its quality of life, businesses have taken the lead in every era with generous support of educational, cultural, recreational, and charitable activities.

In Winston-Salem, these contributions have often been made quietly, as a matter of course and community responsibility.

As much as anything, the profiles of Winston-Salem's Partners in Progress are stories of people and the decisions they have made. Each is a window on our varied and evolving world.

✛

IN 1835 THE BUSINESS LEADERS OF THE MORAVIAN CONGREGATION TOWN TOOK THE FIRST STEP IN MOVING TEXTILE CRAFTS FROM A COTTAGE INDUSTRY TO MASS PRODUCTION. THEY ORGANIZED SALEM COTTON MANUFACTURING COMPANY, THE COMMUNITY'S FIRST FACTORY WHICH BEGAN OPERATING IN 1837. PHOTO COURTESY OF OLD SALEM INC.

Chapter 8

✤

Period I
Pre-World War II

✤

R. J. Reynolds Tobacco Company

RJR's corporate philanthropy has been improving the quality of life in Winston-Salem since RJR was one man's monogram. The young Richard Joshua Reynolds, who rode into the little town of Winston in 1875 to start a

THE DOWNTOWN SCHOOL, AN INNOVATIVE SCHOOL PROMOTING TEAMWORK BETWEEN THE SCHOOL SYSTEM, PARENTS, VOLUNTEERS, AND THE BUSINESS COMMUNITY, IS HOUSED IN THE OLD CITY MARKET BUILDING. AS BUSINESS PARTNER, REYNOLDS TOBACCO PERMITS EMPLOYEES TO TAKE TIME OFF TO VOLUNTEER AT THE SCHOOL AND PROVIDES OPERATIONAL SUPPORT ALONG WITH A VARIETY OF IN-KIND SERVICES.

tobacco manufacturing business, gave his new community more than the thousands of jobs his thriving enterprise created. That same commitment to the community has continued and is present today through R. J. Reynolds Tobacco Co., its employees, its parent company, RJR Nabisco, Inc., as well as the RJR Nabisco Foundation.

Richard Joshua Reynolds was a leading citizen of the town, serving as a

R. J. REYNOLDS TOBACCO CO. SPONSORS AN AFTER-SCHOOL TUTORING PROGRAM IN FOUR MAJOR COMMUNITIES OF THE HOUSING AUTHORITY OF WINSTON-SALEM (HAWS). MORE THAN 200 STUDENTS, THEIR FAMILIES, TEACHERS, AND REPRESENTATIVES FROM COMMUNITY ORGANIZATIONS ATTENDED THE 1994 RECOGNITION CEREMONY AND PICNIC CELEBRATING THE SUCCESS OF THE HAWS AFTER-SCHOOL PROGRAMS.

county commissioner, working with other business leaders to bring much-needed rail service to Winston, and helping to establish a savings bank. Through personal philanthropy he helped build schools, hospitals, and houses to meet the needs of the growing town.

Before his death in 1918, Reynolds had gone beyond the city limits in his support of education, contributing to Guilford College and woman's College in Greensboro (now UNC-Greensboro). His widow, Katharine, continued the tradition, endowing a chair in biology at Davidson College, and giving the city of Winston-Salem $50,000 to buy the land for R. J. Reynolds High School and to build its magnificent auditorium.

The founder of Reynolds Tobacco had a clear understanding that good schools would provide a pool of educated employees for his business and others and would be the foundation of overall betterment of the community. Support of education, at all levels and through many kinds of institutions of learning, has been a focus of the RJR companies' corporate giving and

community involvement for more than 100 years. Many thousands of RJR employees have been inspired and encouraged to give their time, leadership, and money to the causes championed at the corporate level.

Through the 1920s, '30s, and '40s, the tobacco company and its employees made gifts to bricks and mortar projects and to endowment funds at schools, including Buie's Creek Junior College (now Campbell University), Salem College, and North Carolina State College. The following decade was a period of enormous giving, including a $150,000 donation to build a new public library in Winston-Salem. The company and the foundations started by Reynolds family members and RJR employees were a major force in establishing the Bowman Gray School of Medicine in Winston-Salem, and in relocating Wake Forest College from Wake County to the Twin City.

The list of schools and educational programs receiving RJR support through the 1950s, '60s, '70s, and '80s grew by leaps and bounds and numbered new and innovative ventures, including the North Carolina School of the Arts, the Center for Creative Leadership, and the North Carolina School of Science and Mathematics. RJR generosity has also benefited North Carolina State

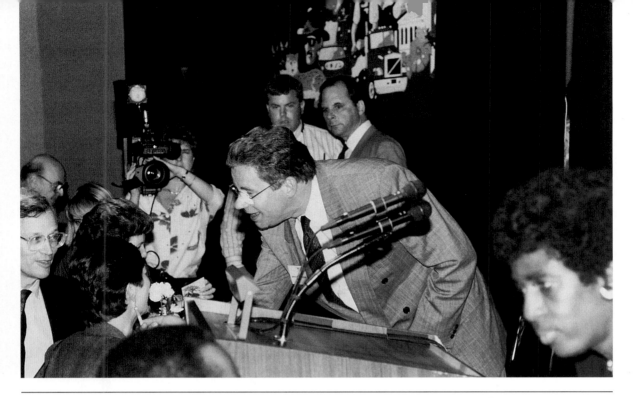

JAMES W. JOHNSTON, CHAIRMAN AND CHIEF EXECUTIVE OFFICER OF R. J. REYNOLDS TOBACCO CO., TALKS WITH GUESTS AFTER A LUNCHEON WHERE THE PIEDMONT TRIAD REGIONAL POSTAL CANCELLATION WAS UNVEILED. SUPPORT FOR ECONOMIC DEVELOPMENT IN THE PIEDMONT TRIAD IS A MAJOR PRIORITY IN RJR'S COMMUNITY RELATIONS AND CONTRIBUTIONS PROGRAMS.

University, Winston-Salem State University, Salem College and Academy, the United Negro College Fund, and the University of North Carolina at Chapel Hill.

RJR support of educational institutions and funds and ventures has been as broad as education itself. Disciplines ranging from agricultural education to minority leadership and student tutoring programs have received support. The cultural institutions that help educate the general public have been the beneficiaries of major gifts. Among them are the North Carolina Zoological Society in Asheboro, the North Carolina Museum of Art in Raleigh, SciWorks, Reynolda House Museum of American Art, and the Southeastern Center for Contemporary Art in Winston-Salem.

Many of the most progressive and enriching programs in the public schools of Winston-Salem and Forsyth County have owed their existence to RJR dollars. One was a program that provided annual scholarships for 29 years to teachers for summer study and travel to keep them current and creative in their fields. Another was a homework hotline service for elementary school pupils.

The company has included its employees in its concern for education, through tuition reimbursements and through degree and certificate programs created by RJR and local colleges.

For many years employees have been given incentives to make personal donations to education and the arts through RJR's matching grants programs.

In the 1990s, as an operating company of RJR Nabisco, Inc., Reynolds Tobacco continues to make K-12 public education and economic development the central focus of its corporate philanthropy. The company is also a solid supporter of selected community initiatives including the United Way and the Arts Council. Reynolds Tobacco strongly supports employee volunteerism in the community. RJR employees serve on local boards and commissions, hold public office, and volunteer in educational and cultural organizations. Through the company's Community Involvement Plan, employees may request financial support for community organizations in which they participate.

Although the changing business environment for the tobacco industry may have imposed limitations on Reynolds Tobacco's ability to continue its financial generosity of the past, the company's commitment to the welfare of the community is still very evident across Winston-Salem and the Piedmont Triad region. ✢

IN R. J. REYNOLDS TOBACCO CO.'S "SCIENTISTS IN THE CLASSROOM" PROGRAM, 24 VOLUNTEER RJR SCIENTISTS WORK WITH FIFTH-GRADE TEACHERS FROM 12 AREA SCHOOLS TO DEVELOP AND IMPLEMENT CLASSROOM RESEARCH PROJECTS CORRELATED WITH SCHOOL CURRICULUM. THE 12-WEEK PROGRAM CULMINATES DURING NATIONAL SCIENCE AND TECHNOLOGY WEEK IN A SCIENCE SYMPOSIUM WHERE THE STUDENTS DISPLAY AND EXPLAIN THEIR COMPLETED PROJECTS FOR THEIR PARENTS. THE PROGRAM IS SPONSORED BY THE WESTERN TRIAD SCIENCE AND MATH ALLIANCE.

Wachovia

William Lemly was no doubt a peculiar sight as he moved his bank safe and office furnishings from Salem "uptown" to Winston in 1879. A few years earlier, in 1866, Lemly and his uncle Israel Lash had established the First National Bank of Salem, one of the first banks to open in the state after the Civil War.

The intervening years had brought a distinct shift in the community's growth pattern, as the nearby county seat of Winston claimed a rapidly increasing share of industry, trade, and population. So in 1879 following his uncle's death, Lemly closed the bank in Salem and reopened it in Winston, where there was clearly a need for a larger, broader-based local bank to support the expansion of textile, furniture, tobacco, and other business enterprises.

On June 16, 1879, Wachovia National Bank was born—its distinctive name

PICTURED HERE IN 1889, STANDING IN FRONT OF WACHOVIA NATIONAL BANK ARE (LEFT TO RIGHT) GEORGE BROOKS, JAMES A. GRAY SR., AND R. J. REYNOLDS.

derived from the one given by Moravian colonists in 1753 to the tract of land they settled in what is now the Piedmont region of North Carolina.

The bank opened initially in a storefront on Main Street and by 1888 had outgrown its headquarters, necessitating another move—this time half a block north to the corner of Third and Main.

Changes in banking came quickly, and in 1891 a new form of financial institution was formed. Functioning as a state-supervised bank, a "trust company" could act as executor, trustee, guardian, fiscal, or transfer agent for individuals and companies. On June 15, 1893, operating under the first trust company charter granted by the North Carolina General Assembly, Wachovia Loan and Trust Company opened with Francis Henry Fries as its new president.

Under Fries' astute leadership, Wachovia Loan and Trust flourished, and in 1911, it merged with Wachovia National Bank—then led by James A. Gray—to form Wachovia Bank and Trust Company. The city's first seven-story "skyscraper," located on the former Wachovia National site at Third and Main, became the combined company's first home. In 1966, it moved into a new 30-story headquarters diagonally across the street. In 1994, Wachovia began construction of a new headquarters—a 28-story, 600,000-square-foot, dome-topped tower of granite and glass located at Second and Main.

Although each of Wachovia's headquarters buildings has been within a block of where the bank was founded, the bank has expanded far beyond its hometown base to become a $36 billion interstate organization internationally recognized for its financial strength and stability. By adding leading banks based in Atlanta and Columbia, South Carolina, Wachovia now has some 500 bank offices in more than 200 cities throughout the Carolinas and in Georgia—where the corporation also maintains a headquarters.

Domestic corporate service offices in Chicago and New York, international representative offices in New York, London, and Tokyo, and residential mortgage offices in Florida, Georgia,

and both Carolinas also bear the Wachovia name.

Although geographic boundaries and services have expanded, Wachovia's roots remain firmly planted in this community. Wachovia's leaders have fostered the belief that the practical, industrious Moravians who founded Salem left the organization a legacy that embodies the desired characteristics of individuals now associated with Wachovia.

"They were creative, disciplined, hardworking people who struggled hard and built much, but also enjoyed music, read books, and basked in the beauty of good furniture, handsome millwork, and good paintings," according to L. M. "Bud" Baker, Wachovia Corporation's CEO. "In this great institution, we still covet hard work, families, high principles, the creative mind, the discipline of excellence, the joy of achievement, and freedom for the spirit and soul of individuals."

Wachovia's business philosophy encompasses these high standards. Its focus is on tailoring a broad array of banking services to meet the needs of its customers, which range from individuals to small businesses, from municipalities, educational, and charitable institutions to large multinational corporations throughout the nation and abroad.

In addition to serving the banking needs of many of the city's individuals, businesses, and institutions and being one of its largest employers, Wachovia and its staff serve the Winston-Salem community in a variety of other ways, from economic development activities to educational, arts, and other community projects.

Wachovia's long-standing relationship with Winston-Salem underscores a mutually beneficial appreciation and understanding of one another; it is a relationship that will continue to guide Wachovia as it explores new banking and social challenges and opportunities in the years ahead. ✤

Winston-Salem State University

From its beginnings as a one-room school to its centennial celebration as a diverse and thriving university, Winston-Salem State University has moved through history with a strong sense of purpose.

It began with the vision of Dr. Simon Green Atkins, an outstanding teacher who came to Winston in 1890 to be principal of Depot Street School. Believing that home ownership was essential to improving the life of black people, Atkins set about developing a black residential neighborhood, Columbian Heights. By 1892, enough families had moved into the neighborhood to justify building a school, and

IN ADDITION TO THE TYPICAL ACADEMIC COURSES TAUGHT IN ALL PUBLIC SCHOOLS, SLATER INDUSTRIAL ACADEMY OFFERED TRAINING IN CARPENTRY, WOODWORKING, BRICKMAKING, BLACKSMITHING, COOKING, AND OTHER USEFUL SKILLS.

Slater Industrial Academy opened on September 28, 1892.

Atkins assumed leadership of the school in 1895, and except for a nine-year period, he remained its head until shortly before his death in 1934. He was succeeded by his son, Francis Atkins, who served until 1961.

Preparing teachers for segregated public schools was the mission of the institution during the Atkins'

presidencies. In 1922, the Slater State Normal School became the first black institution in the state to focus entirely on higher education, its grade school and high school departments having become part of the city school system. In 1925, the state legislature authorized a change of name to Winston-Salem Teachers College and empowered the college to grant four-year baccalaureate degrees. It became the first Negro institution in the United States to grant degrees in elementary school teaching.

During Francis Atkins' tenure, the school's charter was changed again, and a four-year nursing school was established. After Atkins' death, the college was renamed Winston-Salem State College, to reflect its larger scope, and in 1969, it assumed its present name, Winston-Salem State University.

Winston-Salem State University today, with some 2,900 black and white students enrolled on a 94-acre campus, would be unrecognizable to the founder of Slater Industrial Academy. Today's students are offered more than 70 academic programs, and the university grants bachelor degrees in arts, science, and applied science. Some of the newest degree programs are in physical therapy, business music, mass communications, middle grade education, and sports management.

By the time of its centennial celebration in 1992, and under the leadership of Dr. Cleon F. Thompson Jr., the school was aggressively working to enhance every aspect of its operations.

In the mid-1990s, Winston-Salem State University constructed a 400-student residence hall, an addition to O'Kelly Library, which included the important Diggs Gallery, and the Albert

H. Anderson Conference Center, with its John F. and Lillian B. Lewis Microelectronics Center. A Board of Visitors was established, and the institution was working closely with major businesses through its Partners Program. Students benefitted from academic and cultural enrichment programs, while collaborations with the public schools and a public housing project engaged the university in community outreach service.

Just on the horizon was the construction of a $14.5 million Student Services Complex and a downtown research park, a cooperative venture with the Bowman Gray School of Medicine. The school's athletic teams had brought national acclaim to Winston-Salem State for decades under Clarence "Bighouse" Gaines, athletic director from 1946 to 1990. Beginning in 1994, Winston-Salem State became even more visible in the athletic arena, as the host institution for the CIAA Tournament.

A modern, racially integrated university, preparing students for the twenty-first century, Winston-Salem State retains much of the visionary and progressive spirit of its founder. Caring relationships between teachers and students are still at the heart of the education it provides, and serving and guiding the underprivileged are still part of its mission. For all its history, Winston-Salem State has been the cultural center of the city's black community. At the threshold of its second century, the school was well-established as a vital educational resource for the whole community. ❖

Brown & Williamson Tobacco Corporation

The year 1893 seemed an inauspicious time to start a business. A drop in the United States Treasury's gold reserve had triggered a nationwide financial panic. But two entrepreneurs in the young town of Winston, North Carolina, embarked on a venture then

ON JANUARY 19, 1929, 54 WINSTON-SALEM EMPLOYEES AND THEIR FAMILIES BOARDED A TRAIN. THEY ARRIVED IN LOUISVILLE AND WENT DIRECTLY TO THE NEW OFFICES, WHERE THEY SET UP DESKS AND FILE CABINETS.

that thrives 100 years later as part of a worldwide enterprise with more than 200,000 employees in 80 countries.

George Brown was the son of Rufus Brown, a partner in Brown Brothers Tobacco Manufacturing Co., one of Winston's leading tobacco companies. Robert Williamson was the son of T. F. Williamson, who owned tobacco factories in Caswell County and Winston. Both men had worked in the family businesses, and they were married to sisters. In 1893 Rufus Brown died, and George, then 23 years old, had $10,000 to invest in a business. He invited his brother-in-law to join him.

The new partnership took over Williamson's father's brands of plug and chewing tobacco, developed several new products, hired 30 employees, and began operating in 1894. By the early 1900s, the company had set its sights on expansion and broadened its market and its product line. The company entered the snuff market with several new products, including Tube Rose, which is still a leading brand in the South, and still manufactured in Winston-Salem.

Smoking tobacco was becoming more prevalent than chewing tobacco, and in the mid-1920s Brown & Williamson Tobacco Co. purchased the companies that produced the Sir Walter Raleigh and Old North State brands. In 1926 the company made its entry into the fast growing cigarette market with the Old North State label.

By then, the burgeoning cigarette market was dominated by a few leading brands. In order to compete, the company would need a substantial infusion of capital to increase its production capacity and broaden its distribution. Executives of Brown & Williamson met with Sir Hugo Cunliffe-Owen, chairman of the board of British-American Tobacco Company, which had the intention of purchasing a tobacco company in the United States.

The negotiations were successful, and the acquisition was announced in Winston-Salem on March 24, 1927. Reorganized as Brown & Williamson Tobacco Corporation, the company soon faced the question of where to locate its new manufacturing operations. Louisville, Kentucky, was chosen, and the Brown & Williamson factory built there was regarded as one of most modern cigarette facilities of its time.

The first cigarettes made in the Louisville factory were Raleighs, initially marketed as a premium brand. The price was lowered in 1932, and the cigarette packs included coupons redeemable for merchandise. The coupon feature was also a successful promotion strategy with two brands introduced later in the '30s, Kool and Viceroy.

In the following decades, as Brown & Williamson's products were expanding according to consumer preferences for filter tips, longer lengths, and more choice, the parent company was undergoing a series of acquisitions and restructurings. Most recently, after fending off an unfriendly takeover attempt, the company was reorganized in 1990 as B.A.T. Industries Group, which is strategically focused on tobacco and financial services. Brown & Williamson, the third largest tobacco company in the United States, is one of its principal operating companies.

In the 1980s the company consolidated all its cigarette manufacturing at a new plant in Macon, Georgia. The headquarters remain in Louisville, and the company has leaf processing and storing facilities in Lexington, Kentucky, and Wilson, North Carolina.

After a hundred years, Brown & Williamson's ties to Winston-Salem are secure. The company's original plant at the corner of Liberty and First Streets stood until 1969. Operations were moved to a six-story building at Sixth and Chestnut. Some 145 people are employed there, producing 5 million pounds of specialty tobacco products each year. Over the years, more than 250 million pounds of pipe tobacco, smoking tobacco, chewing tobacco, and snuff have been made in Winston-Salem by Brown & Williamson. ❖

WINSTON-SALEM WAS A LEADING CENTER OF NINETEENTH-CENTURY TOBACCO TRADE.

Weyerhaeuser Company

The formation of what would become the world leader in the management of timber resources— Weyerhaeuser Company—began in 1900 when Frederick Weyerhaeuser and his business partners bought 900,000 acres from the Northern Pacific Railway. By the outbreak of World War I, Weyerhaeuser's company had acquired much more timberland in the Northwest, and in the next few decades it built and bought sawmills and expanded its production of lumber. Fueled by the building boom after World War II, the company expanded to become a national and international producer of lumber, plywood, container board, and particle board. Today, it's not only a worldwide marketer of wood and paper products, but also, through its subsidiaries, of personal care products, real estate development, and construction and financial services.

Headquartered in Tacoma, Washington, the company is the world's largest producer of wood pulp, with a quarter of the pulp coming from North Carolina.

The forest industry, the state's oldest, has been fueling the economy of North Carolina for more than three centuries. With today's worldwide markets and ever-expanding product lines, Weyerhaeuser employees in North Carolina can trace their roots directly to the state's earliest enterprises.

The 575,000 acres of forest Weyerhaeuser manages in North Carolina benefit from the company's massive commitment to research and to environmental responsibility. In 1941 the company dedicated America's first tree farm, beginning a nationwide movement which now encompasses 95 million acres under the private stewardship of 70,000 landowners in all 50 states. Twenty-five years later, it continued its commitment and developed High Yield Forestry, a method for growing

ONE NURSERY IN WASHINGTON, NORTH CAROLINA, ALONE PRODUCES 40 MILLION TREES A YEAR, WHICH FIND THEIR WAY INTO FORESTS THROUGHOUT THE SOUTHEAST.

almost twice as much wood fiber per acre as the yield of unmanaged forests. Today, despite the rising demand for forest products, there is more timber being grown in North Carolina and the United States than in 1920. Weyerhaeuser continues its contribution to forest conservation and growth by making it the company's policy to plant more trees than it harvests.

The demand for forest products is expected to double in the next 50 years. In the years ahead, Weyerhaeuser will be challenged to meet the demand, while continuing to responsibly manage the forest environment. Recycling, too, will become even more important, although it is already one of the nation's largest paper recycling enterprises. And the company is meeting the challenges of energy self-sufficiency by producing three-quarters of its power needs, using wastewater, bark, and manufacturing residues as fuel.

The goals of the company's scientific management and research teams are not limited to forest conservation, recycling, and self-sufficiency. For example, since 1970 Weyerhaeuser has invested more than $40 million nationally into research involving air and water quality. Its research staff numbers 257 scientists and engineers, and 198 technicians supporting them. In 1967 it became the first in the industry to create a corporate-level director of environmental research.

With major facilities in New Bern, Plymouth, Greenville, Elkin, and elsewhere in North Carolina, Weyerhaeuser has significant impact on the economy and quality of life in the state. In the past decade alone, the company has invested well over half a billion dollars in new facilities and other capital expenditures in North Carolina. It directly employs 4,000 North Carolinians, and indirectly provides jobs for another 27,000.

As an involved corporate citizen, Weyerhaeuser has helped finance schools, hospitals, fire stations, rescue squads, libraries, YMCAs, and public television stations in North Carolina and has supported cultural events that benefit thousands. The company has provided land for parks and donated or set aside more than 10,000 acres of forest land to protect various natural conservancies. Some 70,000 acres of the company's forest land in North Carolina are managed for values other than timber, and to protect areas of special environmental concern.

With its outstanding record of both productivity and conservation, Weyerhaeuser is nurturing our remarkable, renewable forest resources for future generations of North Carolinians. ❖

EVERY YEAR, WEYERHAEUSER PUMPS MILLIONS OF DOLLARS INTO THE ENVIRONMENT, SO YOU'LL SEE CLEANER AIR, PURER WATER, AND BETTER MANAGED FORESTS. RECYCLING ALONE USES ONE AND A HALF MILLION TONS OF SCRAP PAPER.

Integon

At the turn of the century the South was still undergoing post Civil War reconstruction. It seemed to George A. Grimsley, then superintendent of schools in Greensboro, that the money from the South all went north. Deciding that an insurance company could keep some of that money home, he launched Security Life and Annuity, the grandparent of Integon Corporation, in 1901.

His brother-in-law, C. Collins Taylor, soon gave up selling chewing tobacco and snuff for P. H. Hanes Tobacco Co. in Winston-Salem and joined Grimsley, and the fledgling company was on its way.

Jefferson Standard Life Insurance absorbed the smaller Security Life and Annuity a few years later, making Grimsley president and Taylor vice president of the larger organization, but within eight years the two restless entrepreneurs left to begin a new venture, Security Life and Trust Company located in Greensboro.

The "war to end all wars" was over and industry was booming. Security's first board meeting was held March 16, 1920, and the first policy was sold that day—for an annual premium of $804. In the next 98 days, from their one-room office, company officers and salesmen wrote $1,176,000 of life insurance—a record never before achieved by a new insurance company.

According to Harry Lewis, one of the firm's early salespeople, in those days just after World War I, the hardest thing to sell was the idea of insurance, but "once an agent had gotten across to a prospect the value of insurance as protection for his family, he didn't have too much trouble selling Security's product."

The pace of sales, however, was about to get ahead of the company's reserves. Each time $1 million in insurance was sold, $10,000 had to be set aside in reserve. By 1923 the company was digging deeper and deeper into its capital to keep up with new policies, and Security officers knew that something had to be done.

Board members decided that rather than slow down sales volume, they would sell more stock. That was when Robert Hanes, vice president of Wachovia Bank and Trust Company, offered an intriguing deal. He said he could convince several prominent Winston-Salem businessmen to invest $5,000 each in Security Life—if the company would move to Winston-Salem. The move came in 1924 when the company took space in the Clinard Electric Company building on North Main Street.

"Let us pull together in season and out of season for the upbuilding of a great life insurance company and thereby greatly promote the welfare of Winston-Salem, the state of North Carolina, and the South," Grimsley said of the move.

The company survived 1929's Great Crash, but barely. New sales dwindled, and policyholders borrowed or allowed their policies to lapse because they could not afford the premiums. Disability claims skyrocketed. Then Grimsley and Taylor faced down a buyout bid. They had borrowed heavily to keep the company going and couldn't afford to sell. Their health and reduced finances forced them into retirement, but their company lived on with Dr. Fred Hanes at the helm.

Hanes brought in Sam Booke and Tully D. Blair, and the company began to grow again. The '30s were marked by a surge in the sales and management staff and new insurance sold. By 1933 Security's sales once again exceeded its policy surrenders and loans. Egbert L. Davis Sr. was serving as president and treasurer of the company, and Grady Southern had joined Security to introduce building and loan insurance.

The new plan, sold through building and loan associations, brought a surge in business. In two months, 51 associations had signed up with $60,000 in new business, and Security underwent another growth spurt. The company staff outgrew its quarters twice during this period, moving to the Norfleet house on Spruce Street in 1928 and to the Shore house on West Fourth Street in 1932.

By 1939 the company had $50 million in insurance in force. Security was experiencing such growth that plans were begun to construct its own building.

Then came World War II. A staff of women held the company together while most of the salesmen volunteered for the war effort. Security's insurance in force climbed, even during the war years, and when the salesmen returned, their jobs were secure. A "family" atmosphere had developed within the company that continues today.

The '50s brought new challenges. When the new four-story, 50,000-

square-foot home office building was occupied in 1951, Security had the largest quarters of any business in west Winston-Salem, and needed it. With a 50-percent increase in staff, the company was producing ten times the business.

The decade of the '60s saw a name change and further growth. The Insurance Holding Company Systems Act allowed organizations to own multiple companies. Security Life became Integon Life Insurance Corporation, one of several subsidiary companies under a new Integon Corporation umbrella of financial services.

"The times shape the modern corporation," said then Integon president Ed Collette of the change. "Inevitably it must be so, because no company can contradict today's social forces and be successful. While Integon will preserve the valuable traditions of hard work, service, and innovation in the Security companies, there exists a clear understanding that the corporation must grow and diversify."

The '70s was a decade of still more growth. The company was expanding and changing, fast becoming nationally known. On May 10, 1973, Integon joined the select group of United States businesses that met the requirements for listing on the New York Stock Exchange.

In 1974 Integon once again outgrew its quarters and took office space in the First Union Building. A couple of years later plans were on the drawing board for the major office building that now anchors Winston-Salem's Fifth Street.

Integon no longer looked like its parent, Security Life and Trust Company. Yet as the company grew, so did the spirit it had been founded on—the spirit of teamwork, service, and caring at the human level. Customer service was made faster, more efficient, and more comprehensive than before. Benefits to policy owners, employees, and the community increased, and the company

entered the 1980s with tremendous momentum and the new headquarters building.

"You can see all the way to Virginia," said Chairman Collette as he looked northward for the first time from the new building's 18th-floor terrace. "Integon's horizon is a mighty one from here."

During the '80s, ownership of Integon changed hands several times, beginning with its purchase by Ashland Oil Corporation in 1981 and ending with the purchase in 1990 by Integon Partners, made up of Head Insurance Investors LP and Jupiter Industries. These moves have positioned Integon for even greater growth in the next decade.

Early 1992 saw a reorganization of the company and the sale of all the non-property and casualty operations to Integon Partners II. What remained, the company took public, making the current Integon Corporation a property and casualty insurance holding company with four subsidiaries and a premium finance company under its umbrella.

These national moves have not interfered with Integon's commitment to Winston-Salem and its tradition of community service. "We made a commitment to downtown Winston-Salem in the late '70s with the construction of an 18-story building," said Integon Corporation President James T. Lambie. "I am proud to say that commitment continues, with the construction of a 6-story office and parking deck complex in 1992 and, more recently, the 'MudPies' day care center we built to provide quality child care services to our employees and employees of other companies in the downtown area."

The Integon companies' tradition of community involvement and support goes well beyond brick and mortar though. Corporate contributions to United Way in '92 and '93 were doubled, and Integon people actively participate on local service boards and

agencies throughout the city. A corporate foundation of Integon officers and employees oversees Integon's financial support for human service agencies, the arts, and education.

Lambie said he sees Integon Corporation continuing to grow and expand its property and casualty operations in the next decade. "Plans are underway to expand into eight or nine more states in addition to the six states we are in already," Lambie said, "and I see that expansion continuing even beyond those states in the next 10 years, which means additions to the employment base here in Winston-Salem."

And with that expansion, Lambie also sees the spirit of service to the community growing. "I think you find a real spirit here among all Integon employees, a spirit of cooperation to get the job done and also a spirit of providing the best possible service that we can to insureds and agents. It's a kind of contagious thing. It's something I think has grown out of the kind of people who live in this area and the surrounding counties. People who believe in giving a good day's work for a day's pay. But at the same time, people who are friendly and congenial and get along well with others. I think we are blessed in this area with that base of people to draw from, and I think Integon's total employee force reflects that."

"Integon has changed from what the company was like even five years ago, but that central core spirit we have had over the years still has not changed." ❖

MudPies day care center provides quality child care services to Integon employees and employees of other companies in the downtown area.

T. W. Garner Food Co.

Thad W. Garner, 17, had been saving his money to go to college when the Great Depression hit. Although he had made $600 stoking fires in a one-room school house, delivering papers over a 16-mile route, and driving a school bus, the money was not enough for four years of college. His father, Sam Garner, owner of the Yellow Cab Company, suggested his son take some of his hard-earned money and buy a barbecue stand that was for sale near the airport.

For $200 Thad bought the small drive-in restaurant—and a yellowed piece of paper dated 1860, which bore a recipe for barbecue sauce. Texas Pete™ was born that day.

The company's founder likes to tell the family story.

"A traveling salesman, trying to make a living by renting caps and gowns to high school seniors, stopped at the barbecue stand for a sandwich," Thad Garner recalled. "He liked the sauce so much he offered to peddle it along with his caps and gowns."

Word got around.

Thad and his mother began making the sauce they called "Dixie Pig" on a wood-burning stove in the family farmhouse on Indiana Avenue. Sam Garner began traveling North Carolina roads drumming up customers for "Dixie Pig."

They added a Worcestershire to their line; then customers asked for a hotter

T. W. GARNER'S REGIONAL BUSINESS, WITH THAD GARNER AT THE HELM, HAS GROWN OVER THE YEARS, EXPANDING ITS INDIANA AVENUE SITE, ADDING NEW PRODUCTS AND COMPETING WITH NATIONAL BRANDS.

product, and they concocted "Mexican Joe."

But Sam, a strong patriot, wanted the product to carry a North American name, so in a family caucus they decided a move across the border was in order—thus "Texas" and younger son Harold's nickname, "Pete."

Texas Pete is still the company's premier product. Indeed, people in the Southeast don't ask for "hot sauce;" they ask for Texas Pete.

By the summer of 1933 the business had outgrown the kitchen stove, but there wasn't enough money to finance a move. Thad took a long, hot walk from Indiana Avenue to a downtown bank. He had only his yellowed recipe and his customers for collateral. Times were hard. The bank turned him down.

Dejected, Thad's walk home seemed even longer, and he stopped off at William Fisher's auto mechanic shop for sympathy and a drink of water. Fisher was a long-time family friend. When he heard Thad's story, he asked how much money was needed, went into the back room, and returned with the cash.

"I first tried to refuse the offer, then asked what papers needed to be signed and for how much interest," Garner said. "'No papers. No interest. A handshake will do,' Mr. Fisher said. 'I know you'll repay me when you can.'"

With this money, the entire Garner family moved into the vacated Lawrence Hospital on Oak Street. They even took in boarders to help finance the venture. The former hospital kitchen provided space, stoves, and pots and pans to

cook up all the Texas Pete they could sell.

It would be five more years before the Garners accumulated enough cash to open a bank account. They plowed all their profits back into the business.

"We never bought anything on credit, a practice we continue today," Garner said. "The family has always been conservative when it comes to money. Remember, we were children of the Depression."

By 1942 the Garners could afford to build a small plant back on the Indiana Avenue farm site. They abandoned the hospital pots and pans for stainless steel kettles and set their sights on growth.

During World War II, government representatives approached Thad about making jams, jellies, and preserves for use by the armed forces. But, once again, an obstacle lay in the way. Sugar was rationed and the Garners had no allotment.

Thad found a local attorney who agreed to accompany him to the office in Charlotte where allotments were meted out.

"Family members pooled their gas coupons for the trip," Thad recalled. "The attorney introduced me to the man in charge of saying who got what

TEXAS PETE IS STILL THE COMPANY'S PREMIER PRODUCT. PEOPLE IN THE SOUTHEAST DON'T ASK FOR "HOT SAUCE"; THEY ASK FOR TEXAS PETE.

allotments—like sugar—in the South during the war. I got nervous as the conversation appeared to hit on every subject except a sugar allotment. Finally the man pushed a button on his desk, his secretary appeared, and he dictated an order for me to get as much sugar as I needed. And I returned to Winston-Salem elated."

But the story does not end there. "A few days later, we received a heart-stopping bill from the attorney," Thad said. "I called to inquire if there had not been a mistake. 'No mistake, Son,' the attorney said. 'I had to use a goodly amount of my influence for you—influence that I cannot use again.' I understood, thanked him, and promptly and gratefully paid the bill."

Now the small company had sugar but needed additional equipment. Accustomed to overcoming challenges, Thad built a peach peeler, a washer, and a filling machine, a labeling machine, and a cooling machine, and the Garners were into jellies and jams.

Thad incorporated his company in 1946, making his father and younger brothers, Harold and Ralph, equal partners.

The regional business, with Thad at the helm, has grown over the years, expanding its Indiana Avenue site, adding new products and competing with national brands—sometimes literally in the trenches.

Another of the family's favorite stories came out of the Desert Storm conflict.

"After failing to get support from several other hot-sauce manufacturers, a volunteer group called to see if T. W. Garner Food Company would donate some hot sauce for gift bags to be sent to our soldiers in Saudi Arabia and,

of course, we did," Thad's daughter, Kathryn, said. "We even opened the cartons and sent Texas Pete Sauces, NASCAR Racing hats, and T-shirts to the soldiers as packing material. It was fun later to see on television bottles of Texas Pete sitting in desert tents."

A follow-up to that story came after the conflict when Kathryn Garner heard General Colin Powell say in a television interview that peanut butter and jelly sandwiches were his favorite. She promptly wrote, thanking him for his service to the country and sending his family a gift box of sauces and jellies.

Powell responded, thanking Garner for the box of food products and for sending Texas Pete to his troops. And before the general retired, he repaid the company's favor to his troops in a more lucrative way.

When Garner products were suddenly not reordered for military bases in the early '90s, an investigation revealed that military buyers had unilaterally decided to buy only from companies with national production and distribution systems.

"We made General Powell aware of the situation, and he was instrumental in helping us and other regional companies across the country to regain our fair share of the military food business," Kathryn Garner reported. "Believe me, we hated to see General Powell retire."

A tour of T. W. Garner Food Company today will find multi-thousand-gallon vats of pepper mash and vinegar aging, the aroma of various sauces and the sweet smell of assorted jams and jellies filling the air, a modern research kitchen, computers

A TOUR OF T. W. GARNER FOOD COMPANY TODAY WILL FIND MULTI-THOUSAND-GALLON VATS OF PEPPER MASH AND VINEGAR AGING, A MODERN RESEARCH KITCHEN, COMPUTERS DIRECTING ROWS OF TEXAS PETE HOT SAUCE BOTTLES ALONG A CONVEYOR BELT—AND GARNER FAMILY MEMBERS HARD AT WORK.

directing rows of Texas Pete Hot Sauce bottles along a conveyor belt—and Garner family members hard at work.

A walk through grocery stores from the Atlantic to the Rio Grande will find shelves of barbecue and buffalo wing, hot dog chili, chili no beans, honey mustard, pepper, and seafood sauces and a comprehensive line of Garner's jams, jellies, and preserves—and of course Texas Pete Hot Sauce, The Sauce with Championship Flavor™, which even Texans would like to claim.

Hard work got the family through the Great Depression, and hard work will keep them going. Thad and younger brother Ralph, working with the next generation of Garners, are meeting their obstacles on Indiana Avenue and moving toward the future. Family members involved in the company now, in addition to Thad's daughter, Kathryn, include Ralph's son and daughter, Reg Garner and Ann G. Riddle, and late brother Harold Garner's son, Harold Jr. ❖

DURING WORLD WAR II, GOVERNMENT REPRESENTATIVES APPROACHED THAD GARNER ABOUT MAKING JAMS, JELLIES, AND PRESERVES FOR USE BY THE ARMED FORCES. TODAY, A WALK THROUGH GROCERY STORES FROM THE ATLANTIC TO THE RIO GRANDE WILL FIND SHELVES OF A COMPREHENSIVE LINE OF GARNER'S PRODUCTS.

Krispy Kreme Doughnut Corporation

She took three dozen piping hot Krispy Kremes on the plane with her. The familiar, fresh-from-the-bakery smell drove the other travelers mad. They begged; she shared. The daughter in Chicago for whom she bought the doughnuts got short-changed. "But what the heck," she said. "Mom made a lot of new friends with the Krispy Kremes."

During Desert Storm, it took weeks for Krispy Kremes mailed by a loving mother to her son to arrive at his camp in Saudi Arabia. But homesick Southern soldiers ate them anyway and wished they had more.

And when a new Krispy Kreme store opened, crowds formed an hour early to devour the first hot, glazed doughnuts coming off the line.

All this for a doughnut? Not just any doughnut—a Krispy Kreme.

For more than a half century, these confectionary creations have been a favorite in the South. The taste—the smell—the fragile texture. Krispy Kremes. The mere mention of the name in a far-flung place to another Southerner creates comradery quicker than a secret handshake or a shared childhood experience. Ah, Krispy Kremes.

In 1937 when Vernon Rudolph opened his first doughnut shop in Winston-Salem, he never envisioned

that his small business, the Krispy Kreme Doughnut Company, would evolve into one of the world's largest producers of the delectable treats. Tobacco and textiles were kings, and the business climate was favorable when he arrived in Winston-Salem in a year-old Pontiac, $225 in cash, a few pieces of equipment, and a still-secret recipe for Krispy Kremes.

Rudolph soon convinced a local grocer to lend him the ingredients for a batch of doughnuts and promised to pay him back when the first confections were sold. The backseat of his car came out and boxes of doughnuts went in. The Pontiac that had brought Vernon Rudolph from Kentucky became his delivery vehicle. The doughnuts sold, the debt was repaid, and he was in the wholesale doughnut business for keeps.

It didn't take long for the retail business

VERNON RUDOLPH FOUNDED KRISPY KREME AS A WHOLE-
SALE BUSINESS DELIVERING DOUGHNUTS TO SUPERMAR-
KETS IN THE SOUTHEAST.

to develop, also. Persons driving by smelled doughnuts cooking and stopped to ask if they could buy them. Rudolph responded to customer demand; he cut a hole in the wall and passed them through, piping hot. Krispy Kreme's first "drive-through/walk-up" window was created. Today, bright-red neon "Hot Doughnuts Now" signs in the windows of Krispy Kreme stores constantly remind customers that Krispy Kreme is making fresh, hot doughnuts and serve as a siren call to passing motorists.

That's history, and Krispy Kreme is still making it. From that quiet beginning almost 60 years ago, Krispy Kreme has become the largest maker of yeast-raised doughnuts in the world, serving customers throughout the Southeast and Midwest. Most of the company's production is still wholesale, but retail sales, which began by accident, now are an integral part of Krispy Kreme's development strategy.

Some 85 percent of Krispy Kreme customers want doughnuts to take to the office or home. Consequently, its Express stores, which are only one-third the size of many previous outlets, have two drive-through windows and walk-in, take-out counters with no booths. Despite their size, they can still turn out 150 dozen doughnuts an hour. Its high-tech production lines have become such a curiosity that stores now are specially designed so drive-through customers can watch the doughnut-making process from beginning to end—from mixing dough to cooling the Krispy Kremes.

Krispy Kreme's management team is high-energy and has a vision for the

future. While insuring the day-to-day profitability of the company and aggressively plotting its future, management also devotes time and resources to giving back to Winston-Salem and other communities which have supported Krispy Kreme so well.

In Winston-Salem, Joseph McAleer, the company's chief executive officer, serves on the board of Old Salem Inc. and has donated time of Krispy Kreme lab professionals to make the restoration's showplace, Winkler Bakery, more efficient. Scott Livengood, president, has become a driving force in the work of Habitat for Humanity. Krispy Kreme has bought and donated land to Habitat and made other donations. Company employees have helped build a house for a deserving family. In addition, Krispy Kreme, in partnership with Home Moravian Church, has built a house for a needy family. "We believe in giving back to a community that has supported us so well," said Barbara Thornton, Krispy Kreme's vice president of human resources.

The company is in partnership with Cook Middle School, giving of employee time, energy, and company resources to it and other schools in the area, and participates in United Way, the Crosby tournament, which plows much of its winnings back into the community, and in other charitable organization giving.

"Krispy Kreme is a well-kept secret in town," Thornton said. "Many people do not realize how large we are or our involvement in this community." ✥

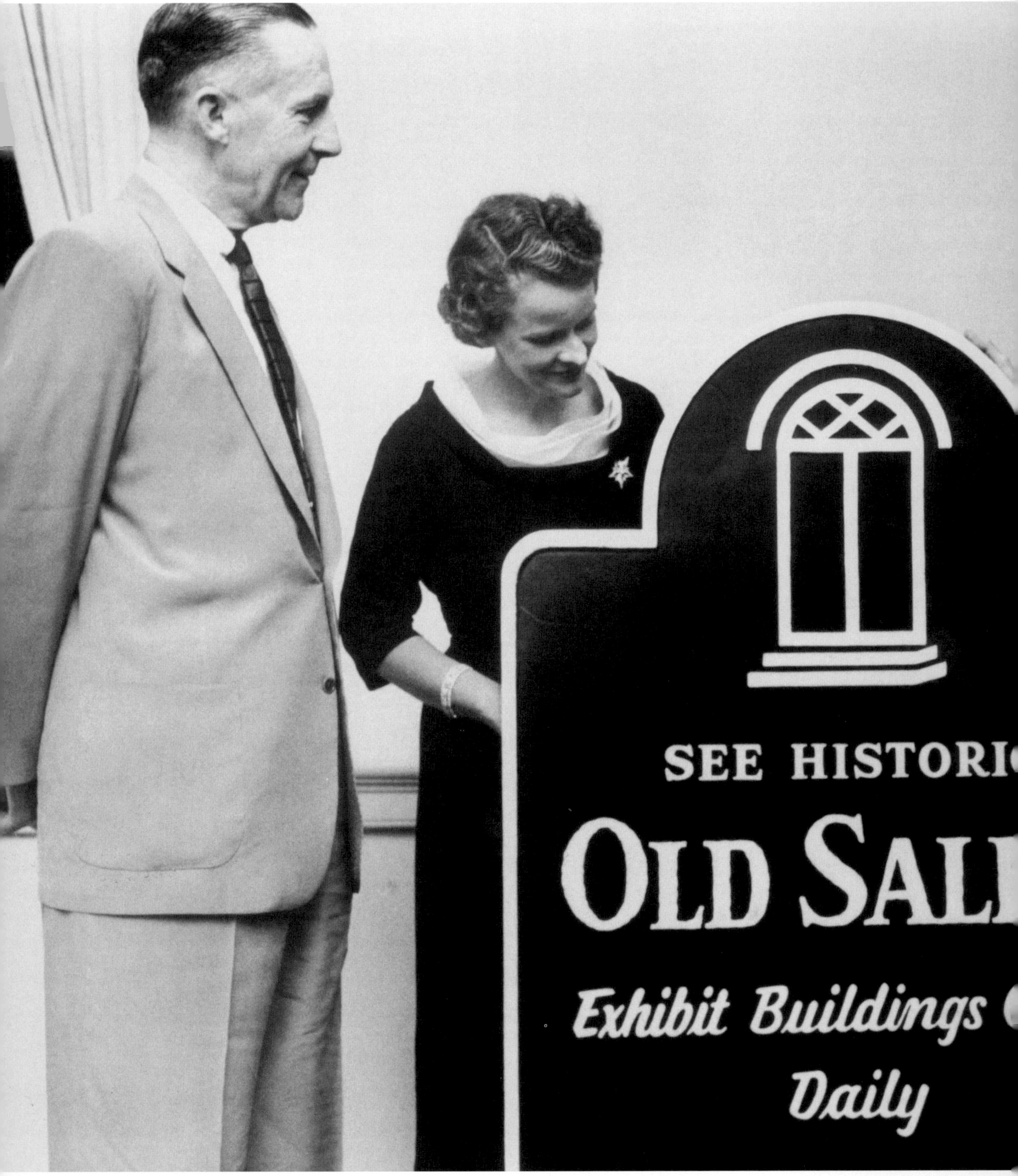
SEE HISTORI
OLD SAL
Exhibit Buildings
Daily

Chapter 9

✥

Period II
(1945-1969)

✥

Alex Brown & Sons, Incorporated

Innovation tempered with tradition is the Alex. Brown & Sons Incorporated approach to doing business. Although the Firm did not begin providing investment services from its Winston-Salem branch until 1946, the parent company, headquartered in Baltimore, Maryland, has been managing and influencing the financial activities of municipalities, companies, and individuals for nearly 200 years.

Traditions are expected at a company with such a long and successful history. At Alex. Brown & Sons, however, traditions focus on maintaining a time-tested commitment to excellence and integrity while pursuing innovative, yet secure, approaches to making money work as productively as possible.

Chairman Emeritus Benjamin H. Griswold IV defined tradition simply in an interview that appeared in *Securities Industry Management,* Summer 1993: "What we call tradition are the value systems or learned lessons of history that have developed over the years. They are characteristics, such as quality, placing the client's interest before your own collegiality, having a very solid capital base, and being innovative. . . . Tradition is not looking backward for answers, and it's not relying on an old-boy network; business is too competitive for that."

Since its inception, the Firm has established a tradition of remaining on the cutting edge of the world of finance, offering its clients and the communities it serves an unparalleled expertise in investment banking.

Investment banking began in the United States in 1810 with Alex. Brown & Sons' underwriting of a $250,000 equity issue for the Baltimore Water Company and distributing this stock to individuals, insurance companies, and other businesses.

The Firm's financing of the fledgling B&O (Baltimore and Ohio) Railroad ushered in the passenger railroad era and was critical to the country's expansion toward the West. In the 1930s the firm produced the first plan for the tax-free financing of Maryland's toll bridges and roads.

A publicly held company traded on the New York Stock Exchange, Alex. Brown & Sons continues today to assist municipalities of all sizes in financing vital infrastructure projects at the most favorable rates.

The stability and security for which Alex. Brown & Sons, the oldest investment bank in the United States, prides itself is evident in the management history of the Winston-Salem branch. John Davis III is only the third manager of the local Firm. Jim Holmes, the second manager, is still active in the company, and the son of the first manager, Ben Willis, also works here. In addition, Chairman Emeritus Ben Griswold IV is the great, great, great grandson of Alexander Brown, who established the firm in 1800. This thread running through the generations is characteristic of the company.

Industries in which the firm has developed specialized coverage include

financial services, real estate, consumer, environmental, health care, media/communications, technology, and transportation. A team of two or more experienced analysts are assigned to follow each industry.

Another characteristic is the Firm's commitment to growth without sacrificing its dedication to quality service. Most of the company's branch offices have relatively few associates. The local office employs 18 professionals and a support staff of 11. The Winston-Salem office is primarily equity driven, but has a longstanding record of success in North Carolina municipal bond business. Additionally, the office has generated substantial business through real estate investments.

BENJAMIN H. GRISWOLD IV, CHAIRMAN EMERITUS OF ALEX. BROWN INCORPORATED, IS A SEVENTH GENERATION DESCENDANT OF THE FIRM'S FOUNDER, ALEXANDER BROWN.

Alex. Brown said, "Remain a prudent and reflective firm holding only to the highest standards of integrity." That philosophy is what continues to drive the company today. Proud of, but not resting on its past or present successes, Alex. Brown & Sons Incorporated looks forward to continued growth—for its clients and for itself—into the next century.

The staff at the Winston-Salem offices looks forward to enjoying many more decades of serving this region with the same time-tested dedication to excellence and integrity found throughout the Firm. ❖

IN 1828, ALEX. BROWN LED THE FIRST OFFERING OF STOCK FOR THE B&O RAILROAD COMPANY. TWO YEARS LATER, ALEXANDER BROWN AND HIS SON GEORGE BROWN MADE THE FIRST JOURNEY IN AMERICA BY STEAM, PULLED IN AN OPEN CAR AT 12 MILES PER HOUR BY THE LOCOMOTIVE "TOM THUMB." PHOTO OF REPLICA COURTESY OF B&O RAILROAD MUSEUM, INC.

Hubbard Realty

The announcement of the 1994 opening of Oak Valley Residential and Golf Community, Davie County's largest residential neighborhood in several decades, was a fitting kickoff for Lewis Hubbard's 44th year in real estate. Oak Valley serves as a scale model of, and a testament to, Hubbard's formula for success in business, combining the resources and capabilities of Hubbard family members with several longtime partners.

LEWIS HUBBARD'S PHILOSOPHY IS "IF YOU HAVE INTEGRITY, AMBITION, AND ABILITY, YOU CAN MOVE MOUNTAINS." THE PEOPLE WHO FORM HUBBARD REALTY HAVE HEARD THIS ADAGE AND HAVE TAKEN IT TO HEART, GEOMETRICALLY MULTIPLYING THE CAPABILITIES OF LEWIS HUBBARD. PHOTO COURTESY OF **WINSTON-SALEM JOURNAL**.

"My father told me as a young man, 'Son, if you have integrity, ambition, and ability, you can move mountains.'" In retrospect it appears that Lewis, already self-supporting at age 12, took the advice literally—mountains of Piedmont pacolyte clay have been moved over the ensuing four decades, providing housing for more than 5,000 families in 100 neighborhoods in Forsyth, Davie, and Davidson counties.

Hubbard is the first to protest that all of this has not been accomplished alone, and therein lies the insight into the founder of Hubbard Realty of Winston-Salem, Inc. Today the organization comprises a sales division of 80 associates, relocation services, insurance, property management, commercial sales, and leasing and development divisions, as well as close work-ing relationships with more than 60 independent homebuilders. Hubbard Realty is assuredly a whole greater than the man and wife who opened shop in the lobby of the Zinzendorf Hotel in 1950. Lewis and Emma Hubbard's children grew up in and with the family business, and their participation has only enhanced the sense of all in the company of being part of a "family." Most, if not all, of the people who form this organization have heard the adage in an early encounter with Lewis— "Integrity, ambition, and ability"—and have taken it to heart, geometrically multiplying the capabilities of a single man.

Hubbard's first foray into the real estate business was in the post-World War II period, when demand far outstripped supply; builders were in need of lots, as well as guidance, with respect to the type of houses to build. The 24-year-old Hubbard filled the niche and gradually worked his way into the land acquisition and development areas. Relationships with homebuilders matured and expanded; second generations of contractors now work with second generation homebuyers. The impact on Forsyth and surrounding counties has been considerable in sheer volume, with more than 3,000 homes having been added to the housing market over the past 20 years, but numbers alone tell only a part of the story.

Hubbard Realty, as managing partner of the Sherwood Company, introduced the first large-scale planned residential development to Forsyth County, New Sherwood Forest, a 350-acre neighborhood off Peace Haven Road, encompassing condominiums, townhouses, single-family homes, and luxury estates on the old Children's Home farm.

Pennston Corporation, son Bruce Hubbard's development entity, broke new ground with King's Grant, a planned neighborhood introducing the zero lot line concept, enabling cluster development to occur on "topographically-challenged" land. Eldest son, Eddie, through his building company, H&V Construction Company, a longtime advocate of affordable, entry-level housing, initiated a two-story home with an unfinished upper level to open the new housing market to a broader range of customers. Daughter Beverly's development acumen has been directed to the sales division with the creation of a professional management team, the introduction of an intensive training program, and a broader focus for the sales division, resulting in sales of existing homes equaling new construction volume.

Hubbard Realty offices are now open in Davie and Davidson counties, in addition to corporate headquarters on Stratford Road in Winston-Salem.

But back to the future—the niche, the hole in the market, the innovation—Oak Valley is evidence that the elder Hubbard's advice still applies. Oak Valley's formula is not new; the developers are Hubbard family members and two longtime partners. The concept is new: a championship golf course designed by Wake Forest University alumnus, Arnold Palmer, surrounded by clusters of neighborhoods ranging in size and price to accommodate a broad range of homeowners, all spread over 600 acres of gorgeous Piedmont terrain. Mountains will be moved; believe it! ❖

AS LEWIS HUBBARD BREAKS GROUND FOR A NEW OFFICE IN DAVIDSON COUNTY, HIS FAMILY AND STAFF LOOK ON WITH PRIDE.

Old Salem Inc.

The Moravians who founded Salem in 1766 could boast a religious heritage as ancient as any in the Protestant world. They traced their faith to the Bohemian martyr John Hus. Hus died at the stake in 1415, but the faith survived, mostly in secret, until in 1722 a small group of the faithful in Moravia (in what is today the Czech Republic) sought a haven where they could worship openly and safely. In the spring of that year they found refuge on the Saxon estate of Count Nikolaus Ludwig von Zinzendorf. Here they founded a religious center called "Herrnhut" and watched over the rebirth of the ancient Unity of Brethren. The land from which they had emigrated would live on in the name of their church; in English-speaking countries today all members of the Unity are knows as "Moravians," though most are from other countries.

IT IS THE CONGREGATION TOWN YEARS THAT OLD SALEM STRIVES TO BRING ALIVE FOR THE SEVERAL HUNDRED THOUSAND VISITORS WHO COME HERE EACH YEAR.

The Moravians looked to America as a place where they could practice their beliefs free from persecution. Their first American colony, founded in 1734 at Savannah, Georgia, encountered unforeseen difficulties. Caught between the warring English and Spanish, the peace-loving Moravians soon gave up on this settlement and, in 1740, joined another group of Brethren who had founded a colony at Bethlehem, Pennsylvania. Their reputation as industrious, law-abiding people soon attracted the attention of the British nobleman Earl Granville, heir to one of the eight lord proprietors from whom Carolina received its founding charter. Convinced that these Moravians would help bring stability to his troubled domain, Granville approached their leaders with an offer of land. An exploratory expedition led to the purchase of a 98,985-acre tract in what is now Piedmont, North Carolina.

To this land in November 1753 came a hardy group of settlers from Pennsylvania. They spent their first night in an abandoned log hut six miles northwest of the future town of Salem. Around this cabin rose a lively town which the inhabitants called Bethabara (Hebrew for "house of passage"). But Bethabara, as its name implies, was only a temporary settlement, never meant to endure as the principal Moravian town. From the beginning the Moravian leaders had been making plans for a central town in Wachovia; a town where economic development, architectural details, and building setbacks could be regulated as strictly as men's lives.

It was not until 1766 that construction began on the central town in Wachovia—the town that would be called Salem from the Hebrew word for "peace." By the spring of 1772 most of the major buildings planned for Salem had been completed. It was then that a majority of the residents of Bethabara and the government of Wachovia moved to the new town.

As the area grew more populous and as roads improved and governments became more efficient, the highly regimented congregation system of Salem, created partly for the purposes of security and to promote a workable Christian brotherhood, lost both its reasons for being and much of its original appeal. Gradually the old rules were either relaxed or abandoned, and by the middle of the nineteenth century, Salem had ceased to function as a congregation town. It is those congregation town years that Old Salem strives to bring alive for the several hundred thousand visitors who come here each year.

Founded in 1950 when plans for a grocery store in the heart of Salem prodded people into overt action, Old Salem Inc. brought together Moravians and non-Moravians, people with wealth and people of limited means, historians, businessmen, and preservationists. Since then more than a hundred non-conforming structures have been demolished and more than 60 restored or reconstructed on their original sites. There was much in Old Salem's favor: the support of the community, the mass of historic reference materials available, and the number of original (though, by 1950, often obscured) structures still standing.

Now that the biggest part of the work of restoring and protecting Salem's historic buildings and artifacts is complete, the primary mission of Old Salem has moved to the forefront: preserving and interpreting the life and culture of an eighteenth- and nineteenth-century backcountry Moravian congregation town. It is an amazing town—certainly one that can serve as a powerful teaching tool for people of all ages. Along with what they learn by walking Old Salem's streets, taking in the theater presentations, studying the painstakingly restored gardens, and exploring the Boys School Museum, visitors will, through their conversations with the authentically costumed interpreters, be exposed to a variety of important themes as they tour the wide variety of historic buildings.

Old Salem is open all year, and no matter when visitors arrive, the district will be alive with historical demonstrations, many offering an opportunity to

SALEM EXHIBITION CENTER

THE SPRING 1996 OPENING OF "TREASURES OF
THE CZECH PEOPLE, 850 TO 1850" WILL BE THE
FIRST SHOW FOR OLD SALEM'S NEW SPECIAL
EXHIBITION CENTER, WHICH WILL ALSO HOUSE A
CHILDREN'S HISTORY DISCOVERY CENTER.

examine, touch, smell, or participate. Demonstrations are scheduled according to the season. The goal is to maintain historical accuracy while providing visitors with as broad a range of experiences as possible.

The Museum of Early Southern Decorative Arts, founded by Old Salem Inc. in 1965, is conveniently located on the southern edge of the historic district. Visitors follow guides through 19 period rooms showcasing the furniture, paintings, textiles, ceramics, silver, and other metalwares made and used in Maryland, Virginia, the Carolinas, Georgia, Kentucky, and Tennessee through 1820. Presented in chronological order, the tour of rooms begins with a 1690 Virginia planter's home and ends with an 1818 South Carolina plantation house.

The brainchild of Frank L. Horton and his mother, Theo Liipfert Taliaferro, the museum displays, preserves, interprets, and documents the arts of the early South. Visitors experience the enormous cultural diversity of the area, encountering sharp contrasts in time and regional tastes through a tour of representative Southern interiors. Six galleries complement the period rooms and provide the visitor with a close view of additional objects in the collection.

The Museum of Early Southern Decorative Arts is an institution long recognized as the country's center for the study of Southern material culture. Its ongoing research program documents the lives and trade histories of Southern artists and artisans working in more than a hundred different trades.

In 1994 Old Salem and the Museum of Early Southern Decorative Arts

(MESDA) were for the third time awarded the highest honor museums in this country can receive: accreditation by the American Association of Museums (AAM). Of the nearly 8,500 museums nationwide, less than 750 have been accredited; 23 of those are in North Carolina.

"We want the people of Winston-Salem to share our pride in being recognized for excellence by the AAM," said Hobie Cawood, president of Old Salem Inc., the parent organization for both museums. Initially accredited in 1972, Old Salem and MESDA were among the first museums in the nation to receive the honor.

Not content simply to "mind the store," Old Salem Inc. and the National Museum of the Czech Republic have formed a partnership to create an exciting new exhibition, "Treasures of the Czech People, 850 to 1850." The exhibition, drawn from the collections of the National Museum in Prague or from the other museums and historic sites managed by the National Museum, will feature 200 masterworks by Czech craftspeople. None of the objects has ever been shown outside the Czech Republic (which is comprised of Bohemia and Moravia, where the Moravian Church has its roots). The show's spring 1996 opening will be the first for Old Salem's new special exhibition center, which will also house a children's history discovery center. After a five-month run here in Winston-Salem, the show will travel to two other venues in the United States. The special exhibition gallery will, in turn, move on to present other shows designed and selected for their ability to place Old Salem and the Museum of Early Southern Decorative Arts into a greater context.

Along with the generous financial support of individuals, businesses, and philanthropic institutions, the non-profit

Old Salem Inc. supports its work with admission income, museum shop and catalog revenues, and royalties from a thriving museum product licensing program. Winkler Bakery continues to create what must be some of the tastiest museum products in the world. T. Bagge-Merchant, the museum shop on the square, is a sure-bet stop for museum visitors and local shoppers alike. The 1994 remodeling of the Visitor Center brought with it the expansion of the popular Old Salem Shop. Lexington Furniture's line of furnishings reproduced from or inspired by the collection is displayed and sold in a beautiful (and historic) house in the heart of the district. The Old Salem Tavern serves hearty Moravian-style fare, and the bed and breakfast inn across the street entices many visitors to stay the night.

Picturesque neighborhood, hard-to-beat bakery, pioneer in historic preservation, important living history site, valued garden restoration resource, world-renowned decorative arts research center, popular tourist attraction—Old Salem is all that and more. ❖

THE MUSEUM OF
EARLY SOUTHERN
DECORATIVE
ARTS DISPLAYS,
PRESERVES,
INTERPRETS, AND
DOCUMENTS THE
ARTS OF ALL THE
EARLY SOUTH.

WXII

Channel 12 went on the air on September 30, 1953, with the first game of the World Series. The New York Yankees beat the Brooklyn Dodgers that day, and Triad viewers got a preview of a television station's commitment and service.

"We weren't quite prepared to go on the air, but it was important that we do so one way or the other," recalled John Comas, who was vice president for programming in 1953. "We shorted out a lot of stuff and got on. We had a little failure during the game but were able to correct it and get back on."

WSJS, the third VHF station to take to the Carolina airwaves, was created through a merger of applications by Gordon Gray's Triangle Broadcasting and the actress Mary Pickford. Both groups had applied for a channel in the area and decided to join forces to get FCC approval.

Pickford eventually sold her interest to Triangle, and the station set a direction that has led to top ratings from the industry and from the community.

An NBC affiliate operating under the call letters WSJS-TV, the station shared quarters with WSJS Radio at 419 Spruce Street until new offices and studios were constructed at 700 Coliseum Drive in 1966. The early transmission tower was located in Kernersville.

"Our facilities on Spruce Street were very cramped," Comas recalled. "Our background scenes were painted on huge window shades. We had a series of rollers coming out of the wall and pulled them up and down as we needed to change the scene. The camera was shooting the same area all the time, but the scenes were different."

Comas also recalled the early practice of whisking tops for the studio's one

table back and forth during station breaks and using mirrors to give depth and variety to camera shots.

Early television staff members were hired for their diversity. An individual might be called on to run the camera for one show, direct another, and give the news on a third. Cramped quarters and a small staff did not, however, keep WSJS from fulfilling its mission—service to the community.

As events occurred that invited television coverage, the creative crew figured out how to get them on the air. Consequently, the crew was outside the studio doing primitive remotes years before other stations undertook such risky transmissions.

They covered the Christmas parade live by putting a cable down the street to catch the activity. And when a heavy snow storm threatened to interrupt worship services at First Baptist Church at Fifth and Spruce Streets, the neophyte broadcasters were on the scene to send the message.

"It snowed for days," Comas recalled. "First Baptist had a revival going on with very important speakers, and the people could not get to the church. We cancelled our regular

THE WXII TRANSMITTER SITS ATOP SAURATOWN MOUNTAIN, 18-AIR-MILES NORTH OF WINSTON-SALEM. THE BUILDING AND TOWER, LOCATED ON 225 ACRES NEAR HANGING ROCK STATE PARK, WERE PLACED IN OPERATION SEPTEMBER 10, 1955.

SINCE THE EARLY DAYS OF TELEVISION, LITTLE HAS CHANGED.

program, and the engineer threw a line from the station over to the church and we broadcast the services."

Of course these "adjustments" to the schedule meant that viewers didn't always get what they expected when they turned on their sets.

Richard Barron, an early vice president of Triangle Broadcasting, also recalled the company's commitment to community service. "The unstated credo of the organization was that we were to do the greatest amount of service for the greatest number of people," Barron said.

Fulfilling that mission, the station broadcast a daily public affairs program. WSJS canceled prime time programming during a ratings week to allow Mayor Red Benton to discuss an important city bond issue. When the new North Carolina educational channel did not have adequate transmission power, WSJS rebroadcast a classroom show for them at 9:00 A.M. The sports staff covered the local Cougars' basketball games in an early attempt to bring professional basketball to the area.

A new transmission tower atop Sauratown Mountain in Stokes County in 1955 guaranteed better reception for the 1,800,700 households in the station's 14-county coverage area.

The move to Broadcast House on Coliseum Drive allowed for technological growth and a larger commitment to community service. The studio, located on three acres, contains 33,408 square feet of space under roof and 2,500 square feet in an open garden court.

The first Red Cross-WSJS blood drive at Broadcast House brought so many donors to the tables in Studio A that the air conditioning was inadequate. The March of Dimes Team Walk, which raised $32,000 in 1981, brought in $750,000 in 1993. In support of its sister station in Des Moines, Iowa, the station

raised $42,000 for victims of the great Midwest flood that same year. In 1992, the station raised $9,000 for the Samaritan Ministries as part of the "Spirit of Christmas." Also, as part of the "Spirit" Drive, WXII collects clothes and toys for families of Appalachia at Christmas time. Kidsfest draws more than 20,000 children and parents annually to a show designed to highlight accomplishments of young people. The "Today's Woman" show successfully focuses on skills and achievements of women.

Under threat of government-mandated breakup of organizations that owned all major news media in a community, Gordon Gray sold WSJS-Television to Multimedia in 1972. At that time the call letters were changed to WXII. In 1983 the station was sold to Pulitzer Broadcasting Company of St. Louis.

Both owners have supported Channel 12's early missions— technological growth and community service.

The station has gone from SuperEye Weather Radar to Stormtrack 12 Doppler Radar and from a video tape machine that took up an entire wall to hand-held sets that ride on photographers' shoulders.

WXII pioneered color broadcasting in the southeast United States. It was the first in the viewing area to offer closed-captioned programming, to obtain a satellite news-gathering vehicle, and to offer a secondary audio program, or channel, on a viewer's screen to broadcast emergency information or to translate audio into a second language.

"We are the most technologically advanced station in the market at this time," said Reynard A. Corley, vice president and general manager.

THE MOVE TO BROADCAST HOUSE IN 1966 ALLOWED FOR A STRONGER COMMUNITY SERVICE COMMITMENT. DONORS AT THE FIRST RED CROSS-WSJS BLOOD DRIVE FILLED THE 33,408-SQUARE-FEET BUILDING AND STRAINED THE AIR-CONDITIONING SYSTEM.

"It's been an interesting ride as we have gotten into the computer age. Pulitzer believes in investing in their properties, and our on-air productions reflect that belief. We are always looking for the next technological advancement or the next programming advancement that we think would fit the audience in this area."

When he looks to the future, Corley also comes back to WXII's commitment to community service.

"We would like to continue to lead in community service and provide a good quality television product for the viewers in this area," he said. "It all goes back to trying to put the best product on the air that we can and serve the community the best we can." ❖

Goody's Pharmaceuticals, Inc.

Headache powders are a Southern tradition. They became popular early in the century for their fast-acting relief of the tough headache pain experienced by textile mill workers. Almost every druggist mixed his own analgesic remedy. Winston-Salem's Martin "Goody" Goodman was one such druggist. He mixed the remedy and, with the help of his young soda fountain employee, Hege Hamilton, sold the powder from his drugstore.

Thad Lewallen Sr., owner of a wholesale candy and tobacco business in Winston-Salem, bought the formula for the headache remedy from Goodman in 1936 and persuaded Hamilton to join his new company as head of production. In a small, two-office setting in downtown Winston-Salem, Goody's Manufacturing Corporation was born.

During the 1930s, Goody's was one of more than 100 headache powders available to the Southern work force. While the Great Depression and competition took its toll on many of the headache powders, Goody's survived.

"Sampling," or person-to-person promotion, has been key to the product's growth and, consequently, the company's growth. Lewallen was legendary for saying, "distribution is the best form of advertising." In those days, Thad Lewallen and his family could be seen handing out samples of Goody's to Southern factory workers at shift changes. The strategy paid off and soon demand for the powders outstripped production.

In 1941 Thad Lewallen purchased the Fletcher Brothers Building—a brick building located in what is now Old Salem. There, Lewallen began the process of modern manufacturing and with the help of a growing and eager sales force, Goody's were soon sold all across the Southeast.

Ann Lewallen Spencer, Thad Lewallen Sr.'s daughter and a board member since the age of 25, became chairman of the company in 1973. In 1992, she was named to the additional post of president and CEO. Thad Lewallen III, grandson of Goody's founder, serves as vice-chairman of the corporation and managing partner of Goody's Holdings, Ltd., the investment arm of the family business.

More than a decade ago, the company began to expand its product line through corporate acquisitions and new product development. Goody's Pharmaceuticals, Inc., formally Goody's Manufacturing Corporation now distributes products such as Goody's Pain Relief Tablets, which were developed in 1982; Isodettes Sore Throat Lozenges and Throat Spray, which it purchased in 1982; OJ's Astringent cleanser, purchased in 1984; and NumZit teething medicine and Numzident oral pain reliever, purchased in 1988.

In 1988, Goody's acquired Mayrand Pharmaceuticals Inc., a Greensboro-based company founded in 1941. The combination of over-the-counter and

AT MAYRAND PHARMACEUTICALS INC., A STATE-OF-THE-ART LABORATORY, SKILLED CHEMISTS TEST THE MANY GOODY'S AND MAYRAND PRODUCTS FOR QUALITY.

ethical pharmaceutical companies allowed for many efficiencies including volume purchasing, warehousing, and distribution. Mayrand's sales and marketing efforts, however, are different from those used for Goody's over-the-counter products. Because Mayrand's products are prescribed by physicians and distributed by pharmacists, and they are marketed by a separate sales force. Mayrand's products include nutritional supplements, anti-inflammatories, decongestants, and other cough-cold medicines and nonanabolic steroids.

Goody's Headache Powders are the flagship brand of the family-owned pharmaceutical company based in Winston-Salem. ❖

IN THE FLETCHER BROTHERS BUILDING—A BRICK BUILDING LOCATED IN WHAT IS NOW OLD SALEM, THAD LEWALLEN BEGAN THE PROCESS OF MODERN MANUFACTURING. WITH THE HELP OF A GROWING AND EAGER SALES FORCE, GOODY'S WERE SOON SOLD ALL ACROSS THE SOUTHEAST.

Wake Forest University

A leader in its community and in American higher education, Wake Forest University is characterized by its devotion to liberal learning and its strong sense of community, fellowship, and ethics.

Founded in 1834 in the rural town of Wake Forest by the Baptist State

IN 1993 AND FOR THE SEVENTH CON-SECUTIVE YEAR, WAKE FOREST WAS RANKED NUMBER ONE IN ITS CATE-GORY IN THE "COLLEGE GUIDE" ISSUE OF U.S. NEWS AND WORLD REPORT.

Convention of North Carolina, Wake Forest is one of the oldest institutions of higher learning in the state. It was exclusively an undergraduate college for men until 1894, when the School of Law was established. The School of Medicine, founded in 1902, offered a two-year medical program until 1941, when it moved to Hawthorne Hill, became associated with the North Carolina Baptist Hospital, and was renamed the Bowman Gray School of Medicine. In 1942 Wake Forest admitted women as regular undergraduate students.

A school of business administration, established in 1948, was divided into undergraduate departments of business and accountancy and economics in 1969, the same year the Babcock Graduate School of Management was established. The undergraduate business and accountancy department was reconstituted as the School of Business and Accountancy in 1980, and the Division of Graduate Studies, established in 1961, is now the Graduate School and encompasses advanced work in the arts and sciences at the College and Medical School.

In 1946 the trustees of Wake Forest College and the Baptist State Convention accepted a proposal by the Z. Smith Reynolds Foundation to relocate the non-medical divisions of the College to 340 acres of rolling, wooded land on the Reynolda estate in northwest Winston-Salem. Between 1952 and 1956, the first 14 buildings were erected on the new campus in Georgian style with what has become Wake Forest's trademark, Old Virginia brick. In the late '50s and early '60s, the Reynolda Gardens portion of the estate, with its lovely woods, lake, meadow, and formal gardens, was deeded to Wake Forest, which continues to maintain the grounds for public use. Reynolda Village, with its array of fine shops and restaurants, also is University-owned. In recent years, a flurry of new construction has swelled the number of buildings on the Reynolda Campus to more than 40. Recent structures include the Olin Physical Laboratory, the Clifton L. Benson University Center, the Edwin G. Wilson Wing of the Z. Smith Reynolds Library, and the new home of the law and graduate management schools, the Worrell Professional Center for Law and Management. The Hawthorne Campus has grown dramatically as well, doubling its space in the last decade alone.

In 1986 Wake Forest severed its formal governance ties with the Baptist State Convention. Today Wake Forest is governed by an independent board of trustees, but its relationship with the Baptist State Convention is an important part of its heritage.

In 1967 the college's augmented character was recognized by its change of name to Wake Forest University. Today, enrollment in all schools of the University totals about 5,400. In 1993 senior Carolyn Frantz of Lafayette, Louisiana, became the institution's fifth Rhodes Scholar, and for the seventh consecutive year, Wake Forest was ranked number one in its category in the "College Guide" issue of *U.S. News and World Report.* The University also is listed in *Barron's Top 50 Colleges, Peterson's Guide to Competitive Colleges,* and the "Most Competitive" category of the *Barron's College Guide.*

WAKE FOREST COMPETES WITH DISTINCTION—ATHLETI-CALLY AND SCHOLASTICALLY— IN NINE MEN'S AND EIGHT WOMEN'S SPORTS IN THE PRESTIGIOUS ATLANTIC COAST CONFERENCE.

Wake Forest competes with distinction—athletically and scholastically—in nine men's and eight women's sports in the prestigious Atlantic Coast Conference.

Wake Forest contributes significantly to Winston-Salem's attractive quality of life. As one of the city's 10 largest employers, the University is a major economic factor in the community. Under the leadership of President Thomas K. Hearn Jr., who was a founder of Leadership Winston-Salem and Winston-Salem, Inc., scores of University students, faculty, and staff volunteer their time in the community to civic, philanthropic, social, welfare, and cultural causes. ✤

WGH*Piedmont* 8

WGH*Piedmont* 8, The Piedmont News Channel, is the ABC television affiliate serving Winston-Salem, Greensboro, High Point, and the surrounding Piedmont communities. So why the unusual name?

The station's call letters stand for "Winston, Greensboro, High Point," but there's much more to its market than that—and much more to its identity as a station.

Years ago the Piedmont was little more than a geographer's term for the area of North Carolina between the mountains and the coastal plain. The three major cities and their suburbs had no more in common with one another than they did with Charlotte or Raleigh. Primitive technology made it somewhat sensible for viewers to watch the television station physically closest to their homes. As in so many things, there just didn't seem to be much choice.

Times have changed. Today's Piedmont is no longer the scattered handful of unconnected communities it once was. To compete in the economic climate of the '90s, regionalism is a must. The 1.3 million people who live in the Piedmont have far more power as a unified force than any one city or county can claim. Our borders have met and begun to blur. People who once were "from out of town" are now neighbors—and they haven't moved.

That's why The Piedmont News Channel has fully equipped newsrooms in all three major cities. That's why it established North Carolina's most extensive news cooperative, The Carolina News Link, connecting television stations from the Appalachians to the Carolina coast, with news operations in 13 cities and 2 states. That's why in the mid-'80s the station adopted The Piedmont as part of its name. And that's why it is no longer logical to watch news that confines itself to just part of the Piedmont.

The people at WGH*Piedmont* 8 know that viewers are busier than ever and cannot always be in front of a television, so they have established a system that lets motorists keep up with the news from their cars or call from any phone to get the latest weather forecast from The Piedmont News Channel's weather lines. They also encourage people who see news happening to dial *888 through Cellular One to let the news staff know about the event.

The station's on-air product reflects that same respect for viewers' time. The morning newscast tells them what's coming up with times to the exact minute—at a time of day when it seems every second counts. Hourly live newscasts throughout the day update viewers on breaking news. The Piedmont News Channel's "First News" at 5 P.M. was the first newscast in the state at that hour.

Recognizing that even at 6 P.M., the traditional time for watching local news, viewers may not be able to focus all of their attention on their televisions, WGH*Piedmont* 8 uses graphics that tell at a glance what each story is about.

And at 11 P.M. there's one thing just about everybody needs at least as much as news—sleep. With "11 at 11," viewers get both. It's 11 uninterrupted

ANCHOR KIM JENKINS COLLECTS CANNED FOOD FROM CONCERT-GOERS DURING WGH**PIEDMONT**'S FREE HOLIDAY CONCERTS. THE FOOD HELPS THE SALVATION ARMY FEED HUNGRY PEOPLE WITH THOUSANDS OF CANNED FOOD DONATIONS.

THE UNITED CEREBRAL PALSY TELETHON HOSTED BY VETERAN WEATHER ANCHOR FRANK DEAL, WITH THE HELP OF NEILL MCNEILL AND CYNTHIA SMOOT HAS BROUGHT IN NEARLY $2 MILLION IN DONATIONS FROM THE PIEDMONT. VOLUNTEERS SUCH AS FRED BLACKMAN AND NASCAR DRIVER GEOFF BODINE HELP MAN THE PHONES DURING THE TWO-DAY EVENT.

minutes of the day's top stories and viewers' first forecast of the next day's weather—all the news in less than half the time. Extended coverage of interesting stories, more weather, and sports finish the half hour for viewers who want to stick around.

"Area viewers drive just about all of our decisions at The Piedmont News Channel," said David Boylan, president and general manager. "That's why we have Contact 8, the market's most thorough and best-staffed consumer-investigative unit." A free call to 1-800-808 NEWS can put a viewer's concerns on the air.

"The Piedmont's been good to us, so we try to give something back," Boylan said. "WGH*Piedmont* 8 wasn't just the first station around to recognize regionalism and its importance; we were also the first to commit to closed-captioning newscasts."

WGH*Piedmont* 8 is deeply involved in community projects. It sponsors The Big Sweep, holiday concerts, "Gifts for Cynthia's Kids," Tour to Tanglewood, Brenner Children's Hospital, and the Telethon for United Cerebral Palsy.

The Big Sweep, a water cleanup program, has brought the Piedmont national recognition with three Take Pride in America awards. Each September, hundreds of volunteers clean tons of trash out of Piedmont rivers, lakes, and streams. NASCAR legend Richard Petty has teamed up in this effort with Piedmont News Channel anchors Neill McNeill and Kim Jenkins.

Each December, anchor Cynthia Smoot brings Christmas to hundreds of children living in foster care or group homes with "Gifts for Cynthia's Kids." Donations of toys, clothes, and gift certificates from individuals and businesses that total thousands of dollars give special children their Christmas wishes.

WGH*Piedmont* 8's free Holiday Concerts in Winston-Salem and Greensboro also have become a holiday tradition. They help the Salvation Army feed hungry people for half the following year with thousands of canned food donations.

WGH*Piedmont* 8 has been the major media supporter of Brenner Children's Hospital since its beginning. This acute-care facility for children is a hospital within North Carolina Baptist Hospital in Winston-Salem. The station's efforts in public service announcements and prime-time specials have created awareness of this unique facility, recruited volunteers, and helped raise more than $1.5 million to help care for children at Brenner.

The telethon for United Cerebral Palsy has been produced by WGH*Piedmont* 8 since 1977. Over the years this two-day event, hosted by veteran weather anchor Frank Deal, has brought in nearly $2 million in donations from the Piedmont and helped to fund the United Cerebral Palsy Adult Center in Greensboro.

AN ANNUAL WGH**PIEDMONT** 8 HOLIDAY PROJECT, "GIFTS FOR CYNTHIA'S KIDS," BRINGS OVER 1,300 CHILDREN LIVING IN FOSTER CARE AND GROUP HOMES CHRISTMAS PRESENTS OF TOYS, CLOTHES, AND GIFT CERTIFICATES.

Great American Communications Corporation, a subsidiary of American Financial Corporation, owns WGH*Piedmont* 8. In the fall of 1993, the station celebrated 30 years on the air in the Piedmont. ✤

WGH**PIEDMONT** ANCHORS, NEILL MCNEILL AND KIM JENKINS AND NASCAR LEGEND RICHARD PETTY PREPARE TO SHOOT SPOTS FOR THE BIG SWEEP, A WATER CLEANUP PROGRAM, WHERE HUNDREDS OF VOLUNTEERS CLEAN TONS OF TRASH OUT OF PIEDMONT RIVERS, LAKES, AND STREAMS.

Westinghouse Electric

For more than 100 years, Westinghouse Electric has written history in America. The company's legacy includes a large measure of vision and foresight, of courage and daring, of perseverance in the face of obstacles.

In his 1986 Centennial statement, former company chairman D. D. Danforth said: "There are few companies in our nation who can look back on a span of 100 years of continuous operation. And of these, there are few indeed whose achievements have contributed so significantly to the industrial might of our nation and the world, to easing the burdens of workmen and housewives, and to making the lives of people brighter and happier."

Company founder George Westinghouse (1846-1914) was a giant in America's early history. Before he turned to the new field of electricity, the entrepreneur had invented the air brake that revolutionized the railway industry and had developed the first automatic railway switching and signaling system.

While other scientists focused on direct electrical current in their research, Westinghouse drew on his experience with electricity in railway signaling and pursued the use of alternating current as a commercial product.

"The launching pad for his alternating current research came at the Chicago Exposition in 1893 when Westinghouse proved the safety and reliability of AC power by lighting 10,000 light bulbs. That's why this country and other countries around the world use AC power rather than DC," said Richard Deem, plant manager of the Winston-Salem Turbine Components Plant.

Westinghouse's first steam turbine-generator was put into operation in 1901. Today—almost 100 years later—the company offers a full spectrum of turbine-generator systems producing from 25 to 1,300 megawatts of power. Since coming on line in 1970, the Winston-Salem plant has contributed significantly to the company's international position.

Over the years Westinghouse has earned a reputation as one of the most technologically advanced companies in the world. The Turbine Components Plant is a prime example of the company's commitment to advanced technologies and modern management techniques in manufacturing higher quality products at competitive prices. It

has turned out more than 2 million turbine blades in 20 years. Blades are the heart of a turbine, used in power generation plants in the conversion of coal, gas, and nuclear fuels into electrical power. Like a pinwheel catches the wind and turns on its pin, blades catch hot, high-pressure steam or exploding gas and turn gigantic turbine and generator shafts to create the alternating current that powers our homes and factories.

"We are the only fully integrated turbine blade shop in the world. If you give us a piece of metal, we can do it all," Deem said. "We can design it and make tools for it. We can forge it. We can machine it, and we can get it to our customers when they need it."

With stainless steel as its primary raw material, the company specializes in very close tolerance products that are critical to the reliable operation of a turbine generator: turbine blades, turbine components (small machined parts), control valving, and repair and refurbishment of various small assemblies.

The Turbine Components Plant also is the only plant in the world that does precision forging of turbine blades.

The Winston-Salem site uses electrical discharge machining and other world-class manufacturing methods throughout the facility. Computer control of production and inspection equipment allows very small tolerances to be maintained—accuracies of .0001 inches, or about the size of a human red blood cell, are common.

"There are all kinds of modern, sophisticated technologies in our plant, and we have continued to invest sizable amounts of money in that technology," Deem said. "Throughout the plant we have modern devices like robots,

COMPANY FOUNDER GEORGE WESTINGHOUSE DREW ON HIS EXPERIENCE WITH ELECTRICITY IN RAILWAY SIGNALING AND PURSUED THE USE OF ALTERNATING CURRENT, WHILE OTHER SCIENTISTS FOCUSED ON DIRECT ELECTRICAL CURRENT. AT THE CHICAGO EXPOSITION IN 1893, HE PROVED THE SAFETY AND RELIABILITY OF AC POWER BY LIGHTING 10,000 LIGHT BULBS.

automated guided vehicles, and artificial intelligence-based command systems."

As turbine technology and customer needs have evolved over the years, Westinghouse has continued to live up to its mission to pioneer innovative techniques, to improve new turbine-generator apparatus, and to extend the life and increase the performance of its customers' existing power generation equipment.

In its second century of service, the company continues to catch the winds of change. It is focused on the goal of remaining the supplier of preference worldwide through a program of total quality—total quality in its products and in its people.

"We don't consider 'total quality' a buzzword; we consider total quality a process that goes on forever so that we can continually improve," Deem said. "The push for total quality has been an umbrella program for everything we do here. It has meant immense improvement in all of our processes, in the shop and in the office. There have been step-change improvements and there have been the slower, continuous type improvements."

Westinghouse has traditionally had one of the largest apprentice training programs in North Carolina at the Turbine Components Plant. During the past seven years, the company has invested more than 6,000 hours a month in training at the Winston-Salem site and has graduated more than 100 certified apprentices in four disciplines.

The plant, which has practiced participative management since it opened, continues to expand employee management opportunities through greater involvement of its teams. The Turbine Components Plant's workers are involved in team-based continued improvement. Teams work on everything from strategic planning and problem solving to quality improvement and community relations programs.

"Teams have the power to give us the competitive edge in a very tough global marketplace," Deem said. "After our commitment to the latest technology, the element that makes this plant more successful than any other is the quality of people we have. We could replace the facilities for a few hundred million dollars, but the skills and dedication of our people are nearly irreplaceable."

Change will be constant with the final push into the twenty-first century, but our focus will continue to be to serve our customers better than anyone else.

It was the Westinghouse commitment that propelled the world into the Age of Electricity. The history of power generation in the twentieth century is filled with technological breakthroughs by Westinghouse engineers—innovations which have reduced the cost and boosted the reliability of electrical power to countless millions for more than 100 years. The Westinghouse power generation tradition is one of continuing success.

The company treasures its tradition, but has never been limited by it. Instead, the Westinghouse power generation of the nineties is driven by renewed commitments to the goals of total quality, employee growth, and customer satisfaction.

These commitments, enriched by pride in past achievements, will push the horizon of progress further. And here in the predawn of a bold, new century, these commitments will enable Westinghouse to pioneer an exciting and promising future. ❖

Chapter 10

Period III
(1970-1994)

Ramey, Inc.

To enhance its quality of life, a city depends on what is going on beneath the surface—its water, storm drain, and sewer lines. Since 1978, Ramey, Inc. has been solving many of Winston-Salem's toughest underground problems and participating in the physical development and expansion of the community.

C. J. "Pete" Ramey and his wife, Dian, founders of Winston-Salem's largest utility contracting business, are proud that their company is regularly called upon to tackle unusual and difficult challenges. When a 100-year-old storm drain under God's Acre in Old Salem cracked, causing the ground

SINCE 1978, RAMEY, INC. HAS BEEN SOLVING MANY OF WINSTON-SALEM'S TOUGHEST UNDERGROUND PROBLEMS AND PARTICIPATING IN THE PHYSICAL DEVELOPMENT AND EXPANSION OF THE COMMUNITY.

MUCH OF RAMEY'S STRENGTH IS IN THE EXPERIENCE AND LOYALTY OF ITS APPROXIMATELY 100 EMPLOYEES AND SUB-CONTRACTORS, MANY OF WHOM HAVE BEEN WITH THE COMPANY SINCE ITS INCEPTION.

to cave in and threatening venerable Moravian graves, Ramey, Inc. solved the problem. When a 48" city water line burst the day after Christmas in 1984, Ramey employees worked around the clock for three days to make the repairs. When the tornados of May 1989 ravaged the community, Ramey people helped clear the debris.

Installing and maintaining underground pipe systems and drains is hard work. But hard work has never intimidated Pete and Dian Ramey. Both grew up in humble circumstances near Galax, Virginia. They married young and moved to Winston-Salem. Both worked for a utility construction company, over a period of years learning all facets of the business.

By age 33, Pete Ramey had the experience, determination, and savings to start his own company. The first "corporate headquarters" was the enclosed back porch of the couple's home in Clemmons, and the first shop was a barn on the property. More important to the Rameys than an impressive image was the good reputation they established with bankers and bonding companies, and the experienced and reliable employees they had with them.

The growth pattern of a utility contracting company is unlike most entrepreneurial ventures. To bid on large municipal projects requires bonding capacity, which is the toughest hurdle a brand-new utility contractor faces. "We had the expertise to do major work, but not the bonding capacity to get major work," Ramey says of the crucial early stage of the company. The bonding companies wanted to see financial strength.

Ramey, Inc. had the chance to bid on a large job in its first year. Unable to obtain a bid bond, the company bid with a certified check for $50,000 and was the low bidder. But to keep the contract and not forfeit the $50,000, Ramey then

had to obtain performance and payment bonds. Again, no surety would bond the job, but Pete Ramey persisted, persuading another contractor to get the bonds for him. Before the bonding agent would approve this arrangement, he insisted on talking with Pete about the project. Subsequently, Ramey got the bonds issued directly to him and made $200,000 on the completed job.

By 1985, Ramey, Inc. had reached $10 million in annual revenues and was moving into new office and shop facilities on North Causeway Drive. Bonding has long since ceased to be a problem—now the company is capable of bonding single jobs up to $10 million and aggregate jobs up to $25 million.

Much of the company's strength is in the experience and loyalty of its approximately 100 employees and subcontractors, many of whom have been with Ramey since its inception.

As the company has prospered, Pete and Dian Ramey have become increasingly involved in the community. Many new minority-owned enterprises have benefited from equipment loans, manpower training, help with financing, and subcontracting jobs from Ramey, Inc. This kind of assistance, like the Rameys' dealing with their employees and the college scholarship they have established in their hometown, exemplifies their firm belief that the best kind of help is a "hand, not a handout."

In his years in Forsyth County, Pete Ramey has come to appreciate the work ethic of the Moravians and feels a kinship with the first settlers of the area. In grading for new subdivisions, an area where Ramey is a major player in the community, it's hard not to be reminded of the first people who shaped this land. He can relate to the hazards of digging into uncharted territory and the satisfaction of building for the long term. Most of all, Pete Ramey admires Moravian industriousness and fairness, a heritage he considers worth perpetuating in his own community. ❖

Brookstown Inn

A fascinating key to Winston-Salem's history is preserved in Brookstown Inn, an elegant bed-and-breakfast hostelry which opened in 1985. For almost half a century the old brick building was no more than a nondescript warehouse, and not until the late 1970s was it recognized as the community's first factory.

In 1835 the business leaders of the Moravian congregation town took the first step in moving textile crafts from a cottage industry to mass production. With the approval of the church elders, they organized Salem Cotton Manufacturing Company and decided to build a factory on the western edge of Salem. One of the stockholders, Francis L. Fries, was dispatched to New England to study textile manufacturing processes. Back at home in Salem, he supervised the construction of the three-story mill which began operating in 1837.

Fries soon left to start his own woolen manufacturing company, and, in 1846, joined forces with his brother Henry to establish a cotton mill, F. & H. Fries Manufacturing Company. While the Fries brothers' enterprises were flourishing, the Salem Cotton Manufacturing Company was floundering. By 1850 it was on the market and four years later was purchased by John M. Morehead, former governor of North Carolina.

The F. & H. Fries Manufacturing Company acquired the company in 1863 and turned the building into a grist mill, which operated until the end of the nineteenth century. By then the original cotton mill building had a thriving addition, Arista Cotton Mill, another Fries enterprise. The whole mill complex was later enlarged again and continued operating as a cotton mill until the mid-1920s.

Francis Fries had died in 1863, leaving his sons to continue his work. Their cotton mill was among the first in the South to be lighted with electricity, and was an important factor in the prosperity of the city, employing about 150 men and women.

Francis L. Fries and his sons were Winston-Salem's first true industrialists. Their mill complex stands as a permanent reminder of the industrial revolution as it was first experienced here. The 1837 building has been restored to a use which makes this moment in history accessible and vivid to hundreds of visitors.

The Brookstown Inn reveals its origins in its brick walls, exposed beams and rafters, and a wide variety of guest rooms. On the fourth floor, which originally served as a dormitory for girls who worked in the mill, a "graffiti wall" on which the young women wrote their names is preserved behind glass. The guest rooms, dining room, and cozy parlor are furnished with an eclectic blend of seventeenth and eighteenth century-style primitive pieces and antiques from the British Isles. Handcrafted accessories and eighteenth-century fabric designs and color schemes contribute to the inn's personal and pleasing atmosphere.

While maintaining the appeal of an earlier era, Brookstown Inn offers the modern conveniences travelers expect, along with many little extras. Some of the big modern bathrooms have whirlpool tubs. This is the setting for complimentary wine and cheese each evening. The remote control television sets are housed in rustic armoires. The handstitched quilts are turned down each night for guests.

But for the diligence of local preservationists, this piece of Winston-Salem history might well have disappeared. In the late 1970s, the transfer and storage company which for decades had used the old mill as a warehouse was ready to tear it down and put up a new building. Restorationists in Old Salem began looking into its origins and realized that this was the Salem cotton mill previously known to them only through written descriptions in the Moravian archives. The plans were changed and the mill complex was listed on the National Register of Historic Places.

Salem was known for its hospitality long before it ventured into mass production of textiles. That older tradition is beautifully carried on today, under the management of Interstate Hotels, at Brookstown Inn. ❖

THE SALEM COTTON MANUFACTURING COMPANY WAS BUILT ON THE WESTERN EDGE OF SALEM AND BEGAN OPERATING IN 1837. FOR ALMOST HALF A CENTURY THE OLD BRICK BUILDING WAS NO MORE THAN A NONDESCRIPT WAREHOUSE, AND NOT UNTIL THE LATE 1970S WAS IT RECOGNIZED AS THE COMMUNITY'S FIRST FACTORY.

WHILE MAINTAINING THE APPEAL OF AN EARLIER ERA, BROOKSTOWN INN OFFERS THE MODERN CONVENIENCES TRAVELERS EXPECT, ALONG WITH MANY LITTLE EXTRAS.

Winston-Salem Magazine

The *Winston-Salem Magazine* plays an important role in recording the history of a community known for its historical significance. The publication's life goes back to 1984 when the magazine began as a partnership between editor Mary Reardon and publisher Dwight Shaw. It continues to grow and mature in coverage under the ownership of present publisher Luigi Bozzo.

By nature, Bozzo is more than a publisher, he's a community supporter, and his magazine shows that. He is convinced that Winston-Salem residents look for one thing in a local publication—community news and features—and they find it in the *Winston Salem Magazine.*

"All that's in *Winston-Salem Magazine*, from the first word to the last, relates directly to Winston-Salem," Bozzo said. "Editorially speaking, we've repositioned the publication in recent years. The magazine was more lifestyle oriented in the '80s. In the '90s things have changed. People are going back to basics and family values and are cutting some of the frills."

The 1980s magazine featured columns about wines, cars, and cosmetics. The current publication instead runs columns about local events, people, and places. Early issues of the magazine frequently had models on the cover. Fronts now feature local people. Any national celebrities that appear have a tie to the area and to area activities.

Added to its community orientation, the magazine can be considered a "good news" publication. "Editorially we tend to see the glass half-full rather than half-empty," Bozzo said. "We look for the positive rather than trying to highlight the negative because we feel in this time of uncertainty and global restructuring, readers appreciate knowing about positive things that are going on."

Born and raised in Italy, Bozzo has been in radio and television broadcasting and published a daily newspaper in that country. He came to Winston-Salem with his wife Maril. She is art director and production manager for the magazine.

Although he admits to a few rough years in the beginning, the publisher is a man who looked at the broad picture and plowed ahead in spite of the economic downturn.

"Our first couple of years were short economically," Bozzo recalled. "When we acquired 100 percent of the magazine in 1990, we were in recession. Retail and corporate advertising expenditures were down. It was a tough time for the magazine publishing business, a hard time to be in, but for us a good time too because we had to restructure."

In that period the magazine changed to a digitalized pre-press operation which allowed the staff to do more preliminary work in-house and go to press at a much later production stage. Those changes, Bozzo said, save time, are cost effective, and result in higher quality.

The change also has allowed the company to expand into other avenues. *Winston-Salem Magazine* now publishes *Triad Family*, a tabloid well received in the community, and produces *Downtown Winston-Salem*, a community newspaper published by the Central Winston-Salem Association. They also produce play bills for local colleges and provide pre-press and printing services for other companies.

Even with the organization's recent expansion, Bozzo expects *Winston-Salem Magazine* to remain the company's flagship title.

"A strength of *Winston-Salem Magazine* has been its quality graphic design and the format itself," Bozzo said. "The best communities are said to be the best informed, and I feel our magazine is an enrichment for Winston-Salem. We are able to understand and inform about the community." ❖

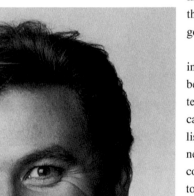

LUIGI BOZZO IS MORE THAN A PUBLISHER, HE'S A COMMUNITY SUPPORTER, AND **WINSTON-SALEM MAGAZINE** SHOWS THAT.

Century 21 Advantage

"Our customers deserve, and will receive, the finest service ever offered by any real estate organization."

Quality is the first priority at Century 21 Advantage located at 2536 Reynolda Road. The company specializes in the sale of residential, single-family homes.

Part of the world's largest realty referral network, Century 21 Advantage is filling the service gap in the Winston-Salem community. With over 6,500 offices, the company accesses a world-wide team of over 80,000 Century 21 sales professionals. They are also members of International Relocation Consultants, an elite group of offices within the larger organization that observes even higher standards.

"In today's global business com munity, families often are required to relocate across thousands of miles, or between countries," Christine Montgomery, relocation director of Century 21 Advantage says. "I understand the emotions and needs of families who are relocating to a new area. I personally handle each referral, assuring that our clients receive the 'legendary,' quality service they deserve."

Realtor John Michelotti, broker-in-charge of Century 21 Advantage, cites Century 21's training program and support system as keys to the company's success. "Century 21 worldwide focuses on quality service, and that's certainly our aim in this office," Michelotti says. "Service is the only product that we sell, and if we can't provide the very best service in our industry, we are not serving our purpose."

The Century 21 Advantage team is a group of trained professional real estate sales associates who take their jobs very seriously. Their goal is to maintain the highest professional standard of any real estate company.

"We make sure each associate is conscious that the attitude of this company is to provide service," Michelotti says. "Our goal is to represent our clients and provide a marketing plan to sell their property within a reasonable time, netting them the most money, with the fewest problems."

The realtor credits the Winston-Salem community and the area Chamber of Commerce with providing fertile ground for the young company and an inviting setting in which new residents can put down roots.

"I believe in Winston-Salem," Michelotti said. "The quality of life here is just fantastic. It's a comfortable place to raise a family. The arts are strong here, and that is an important contribution. And it's a growing community. The Chamber of Commerce has done a wonderful job of attracting industry to the area, and we are constantly growing and opening up single-family communities." ✣

JOHN MICHELOTTI, BROKER-IN-CHARGE OF CENTURY 21 ADVANTAGE SAYS "SERVICE IS THE ONLY PRODUCT THAT WE SELL, AND IF WE CAN'T PROVIDE THE VERY BEST SERVICE IN OUR INDUSTRY, WE ARE NOT SERVING OUR PURPOSE."

NANCY DAVIS, A MEMBER OF THE CENTURY 21 ADVANTAGE TEAM, IS JUST ONE OF A GROUP OF TRAINED PROFESSIONAL REAL ESTATE SALES ASSOCIATES WHO TAKE THEIR JOBS SERIOUSLY. ANOTHER SATISFIED FAMILY WILL PUT DOWN ROOTS IN WINSTON-SALEM BECAUSE OF NANCY'S COMMITMENT TO QUALITY SERVICE.

The Hawthorne Inn and Conference Center

The Hawthorne Inn and Conference Center represents a new frontier in North Carolina Baptist Hospital's history of service.

Located at High and Marshall Streets downtown, the newest member of the Winston-Salem caring and healing community serves a threefold purpose. It offers lodging for business travelers, provides facilities for professional meetings and conferences, and affords shelter and compassionate caring for family members of hospital patients.

The image of its namesake, the hawthorn, and other trees appear in photographic prints throughout the seven-floor inn, reminding guests of the centuries-old role trees have played in sheltering and sustaining mankind.

The restaurant is named The Bayberry. Meeting rooms are called Sycamore and Poplar. The conference room is named for the linden tree. World renowned photographer Ansel Adams and medical center photographer Lee Runion produced the black-and-white images of trees for the center.

The 161-room Hawthorne Inn and Conference Center offers much more than a typical hotel. The hospital bought the inn in 1991 to provide shelter for family members of its patients. After "shelter," the passwords at the Hawthorne are "service" and "support."

While the more than 60 staff members all come from a hotel background, they are specifically selected for their ability to respond to client needs with compassion.

"We believe the medical center does an excellent job of taking care of the patients, and we want to extend that care to their families because we believe families play a role in the welfare of the patient," said Ron Nelson, The Hawthorne's general manager. "Many of the patients and their families come from rural areas throughout North Carolina and surrounding states. We attempt to provide a compassionate attitude in all our contacts with them."

The Hawthorne provides 24-hour shuttle service to and from the medical center on demand and transportation to and from town and shopping malls during business hours.

The inn's top floor includes several two-room suites that consist of kitchen and living areas connected to a large bedroom and two balconies. Arranged to accommodate clients for lengthy stays, the suites have refrigerators, microwave ovens, and a bar for eating. They are stocked with essentials, and dishes and eating utensils are available. Elevators and a wheelchair lift located at the stairs provide convenient access to the upper floors.

THE HAWTHORNE INN'S MISSION IS TO OFFER LODGING FOR BUSINESS TRAVELERS, PROVIDE FACILITIES FOR PROFESSIONAL MEETINGS, AND AFFORD SHELTER AND COMPASSION TO FAMILY MEMBERS OF HOSPITAL PATIENTS.

THE BAYBERRY RESTAURANT, SERVING A TEMPTING ARRAY OF CULINARY DELIGHTS, IS JUST ONE OF THE MANY AMENITIES THAT MAKE A STAY AT THE HAWTHORNE INN A PLEASANT EXPERIENCE.

THE LINDEN, SYCAMORE, AND POPLAR CONFERENCE ROOMS STAND READY TO ACCOMMODATE ANY MEETING PLANNERS NEEDS.

The inn gives the same level of care to its business clientele that it does to families of hospital patients. The modern plum, gray, and green European decor with wood-paneled walls and marble floors invites individuals and groups into a quiet, relaxing setting. A swimming pool and well-equipped fitness center provide exercise opportunities.

The Bayberry Restaurant serves breakfast, lunch, and dinner between 6:30 A.M. and 10:00 P.M., and a complimentary continental breakfast is delivered to each guest daily. All the rooms have coffee makers.

The Sycamore Ballroom, which divides into three areas, offers flexibility for large groups, seating up to 344 people for banquets, 550 theater style, or 220 in a classroom setting.

The Poplar Room, which also divides into three, caters to groups up to 200. Full catering and a variety of meeting-break menus are available.

A small conference room on the top floor affords a magnificent view of Old Salem, a restored 18th-century Moravian settlement and one of Winston-Salem's premier attractions.

Audiovisual equipment, faxing, photocopying, and message services are available for meetings and traveling guests.

The Hawthorne is a short stroll from either the Winston-Salem business district or the Old Salem Historic Restoration, from the Stevens Center for the Performing Arts and from Benton Convention Center.

A short drive or shuttle ride takes guests to the Southeastern Center for Contemporary Art, Reynolda House Museum of American Art, Lawrence Joel Veterans' Memorial Coliseum, Dixie Classic Fairgrounds, Wake Forest University, Winston-Salem State University, North Carolina School of the Arts, Salem College, area golf courses, Tanglewood Park, and major corporations in the Piedmont Triad.

"My experience with The Hawthorne Inn has been excellent," said Jeff Brock, a frequent business traveler to the area.

"From the front desk to housekeeping, the staff is very personable and professional. Services provided with your accommodation make the stay both enjoyable and memorable. In business lingo, we call The Hawthorne 'a solid' for your travel-meeting dollar."

So from corporate clients to hospital visitors, the word goes out, The Hawthorne Inn and Conference Center lives up to its namesake. It brings support, shelter, and strength to its guests and represents the best in quality service and caring in Winston-Salem. ❖

Bibliography

Banner, Leslie. *A Passionate Preference: The Story of the North Carolina School of the Arts.* Winston-Salem: North Carolina School of the Arts Foundation, Inc., 1987.

Brownlee, Fambrough. *Winston-Salem: A Pictorial History.* Norfolk: Donning Company, 1977.

Davis, Chester. *Hidden Seed and Harvest: A History of the Moravians.* Winston-Salem: Wachovia Historical Society, 1959.

Fries, Adelaide L., Stuart T. Wright, and J. Edwin Hendricks. *Forsyth: The History of a County on the March.* Chapel Hill: University of North Carolina Press, 1976.

Griffin, Frances. *Old Salem: An Adventure in Historic Preservation.* Winston-Salem: Old Salem Inc., 1970.

Griffin, Frances, ed. *The Three Forks of Muddy Creek.* Winston-Salem: Old Salem Inc., 1981.

Haislip, Bryan. *A History of the Z. Smith Reynolds Foundation.* Winston-Salem: John F. Blair, Publisher, 1967.

James, Hunter. *The Quiet People of the Land.* Chapel Hill: The University of North Carolina Press, 1976.

Miller, Bertha Hampton. "Blacks in Winston-Salem, North Carolina 1895-1920: Community Development in an Era of Benevolent Paternalism." Diss. 1981.

Old Salem in Pictures. Charlotte: McNally and Loftin, Publishers, 1966.

Rondthaler, Edward. *The Memorabilia of Fifty Years, 1877-1927.* Raleigh: Edwards and Broughton, 1928.

Scippio, Annette. "African-American Community Leadership in Winston-Salem/Forsyth County: A Look Forward." Diss., Duke University, 1993.

Sensbach, Jon F. "A Separate Canaan: The Making of an Afro-Moravian World in North Carolina, 1763-1856." Diss. 1991.

Shepard, Colin W. "The North Carolina Moravians and the Civil War." Honors essay, UNCG-Chapel Hill, 1993.

Shaw, Bynum. *The History of Wake Forest College.* Winston-Salem: Wake Forest University, 1988.

Tilley, Nannie M. *Reynolds Homestead: 1814-1970.* Richmond: Robert Kline and Company, 1970.

Wellman, Manly Wade and Larry Edward Tise. *Winston-Salem in History,* vols. 1-13. Winston-Salem, 1966-76.

Winston-Salem Section of the North Carolina Chapter of the American Institute of Architects. *Architectural Guide: Winston-Salem, Forsyth County.* Winston-Salem, 1978.

Young, Douglas M. *Morobullia: Seventy-five Years of Winston-Salem Rotary.* Winston-Salem, 1992.

Periodicals:
   Business North Carolina
   Carolina Piedmont
   Triad Business
   Winston-Salem Journal and Sentinel
   Winston-Salem Magazine

Patrons

Index

This book was set in Snell Roundhand, Caslon Open Face, Times Roman, and Copperplate at Community Communications in Montgomery, Alabama.